Adieu Derrida

Adieu Derrida

Edited by

Costas Douzinas

The Birkbeck Institute for the Humanities Lectures

First published 2007 by
PALGRAVE MACMILLAN
Houndmills, Basingstoke, Hampshire RG21 6XS and
175 Fifth Avenue, New York, N. Y. 10010
Companies and representatives throughout the world

PALGRAVE MACMILLAN is the global academic imprint of the Palgrave
Macmillan division of St. Martin's Press, LLC and of Palgrave Macmillan
Ltd. Macmillan® is a registered trademark in the United States, United
Kingdom and other countries. Palgrave is a registered trademark in the
European Union and other countries.

ISBN-13: 978–0–230–00714–7 hardback
ISBN-10: 0–230–00714–7   hardback

This book is printed on paper suitable for recycling and made from
fully managed and sustained forest sources. Logging, pulping
and manufacturing processes are expected to conform to the
environmental regulations of the country of orgin.

A catalogue record for this book is available from the British Library.

A catalog record for this book is avaible from the Library of Congress.

10   9   8   7   6   5   4   3   2   1
16   15   14   13   12   11   10   09   08   07

Printed and bound in Great Britain by
Antony Rowe Ltd, Chippenham and Eastbourne

Contents

Notes on the Contributors

Alain Badiou teaches at the Collège Internationale de Philosophie in Paris. His books in English include *Being and Event* (2006), *Metapolitics* (2005) and *Ethics* (2002).

Etienne Balibar is Emeritus Professor at the University of Paris-X. His books in English include *We, the People of Europe* (2003), *Politics and the Other Scene* (2002) and *Masses, Classes, Ideas* (1994).

Drucilla Cornell is a Professor of Law, Politics and Women's Studies at Rutgers University. Her books include *Ethical Feminism* (2006), *At the Heart of Freedom* (1998) and *The Imaginary Domain* (1995).

Costas Douzinas is Professor of Law and Director of the Birkbeck Institute for the Humanities. His books include *Human Rights and Empire* (2007), *Critical Jurisprudence* (2005) and *The End of Human Rights* (2000).

J. Hillis Miller is Professor of English at the University of California Irvine. His books include *Literature as Conduct* (2005), *Others* (2001) and *Topographies* (1998).

Jean-Luc Nancy is Distinguished Professor of Philosophy at the Marc Bloch University, Strasbourg. His books in English include *The Ground of Image* (2005), *A Finite Thinking* (2003) and *Being Singular Plural* (2001).

Jacques Rancière taught at the University of Paris-VIII. His books available in English include *The Politics of Aesthetics* (2006), *The Philosopher and his Poor* (2004) and *The Flesh of Words* (2004).

Gayatri Chakravorty Spivak is Professor in Humanities at Columbia University. Her books include *In Other Worlds* (2006), *Death of a Discipline* (2005) and *A Critique of Post-Colonial Reason* (1999).

Slavoj Žižek is the International Director of the Birkbeck Institute for the Humanities. His books include *The Parallax View* (2006), *Iraq: the Borrowed Kettle* (2004) and *The Puppet and the Dwarf* (2003).

1
Derrida's Eulogy

Costas Douzinas

'What happens when a great thinker becomes silent, one whom we read and reread, and also heard, one from whom we were still awaiting a response, as if such a response would help us not only to think otherwise but also to read what we thought we had already read under his signature, a response that held everything in reserve, and so much more than what we thought we had already recognised there?'[1] This was Jacques Derrida in his eulogy for Levinas, *Adieu to Emmanuel Levinas*. His question is even more pressing for us today: What becomes when Derrida, a great thinker, becomes silent? What becomes of Derrida, what becomes of his friends, those who read him, think through him, speak to him? Some of the answers in the media and the self-satisfied end of the academy, immediately after his death on 8 October 2004, were a depressing reminder of the ignorance, bad faith and banality that dominates so large a part of public culture in Britain and the United States.

The answer of a group of friends at the Institute for the Humanities, Birkbeck College, University of London, was to launch the 'Adieu Derrida' lecture series two months after his death. It was the inaugural activity of an Institute dedicated to intellectual debate on current political issues and to the promotion of the role of the public intellectual. A commentator in the *Observer* newspaper responded to the announcement in a predictable manner. Entitling the article 'What have intellectuals ever done for the world?', the columnist argued that 'by focusing on Derrida, whose work took impenetrability to dizzying heights, Birkbeck is clearly signalling that by "public" it means elitism on a platform.' Intellectuals are inadequately equipped to participate in 'public political debate'. We would 'be better off sticking to Derrida'.[2]

This is exactly what we did. This volume collects the lectures delivered to packed audiences in May and June 2005.[3] They were a huge success despite the snide remarks. They brought together Derrida's philosophical friends and allies and hundreds of people who came to celebrate a *bios euethes*, a life of good ethos, committed to philosophy, politics, ethics, dissent and the public good. The lecture series was co-organised and administered with exceptional efficiency and elegance by Bonnie Garnett. Hervé Ferrage was a great collaborator and gracious host at the *Institut Français*, which sponsored the series. Pablo Ghetti helped with the editing of this volume. Dan Bunyard, our editor at Palgrave Macmillan, followed the lectures and enthusiastically pursued this collection from the beginning. Finally, I would like to thank the many friends at Birkbeck College who helped make the series one of the most important recent public events in London.

***

The lectures were 'posthumous gifts', like the many eulogies Derrida wrote and read for dead friends.[4] They were eulogies for Derrida. Many referred to the personal relationship and friendship between the speaker and Derrida. We have kept in this collection the oral tone of delivery and the auditory emotion they created. **Jean-Luc Nancy** opened the series with an emotional, deeply touching and poetic eulogy to his friend and interlocutor of many years. Nancy celebrates and threnodies the madness of self, of the pronoun *I*, Derrida's madness. It is a testament of philosophical and personal love, an amorous prayer from this most secular of believers. **Alain Badiou**'s personal and philosophical homage salutes Derrrida's *différance* as an attempt to come close to the vanishing point of (in)existence without destroying it. Derrida's death brings to a close a generation of philosophical revolutionary ferment, which included Lacan, Althusser, Foucault, Lyotard and Deleuze. These names remain 'a beacon and lantern' for our confused times. **Gayatri Chakravorty Spivak**'s eulogy takes her back to Derrida's gift, 'as responsibility, accountability' and, to his attempt to mourn the mother. Through an exploration of the relationship between Kant's regulative 'as if' and Derrida's trace, Spivak approaches feminism as the recognition of the 'child-trace of mother'. Temporalisation, giving and taking time, is the mother's gift and it is within that framework that we should be thinking the democracy to come, literalising Derrida against the neo-Kantian liberal cosmopolitans. **Etienne Balibar** offers a paradigmatically Derridean reading of the concept of sense-certainty in Hegel's phenomenology and Benveniste's dialogic constitution of subjectivity. Balibar shows clear continuities between the traditions of dialectics, structural linguistics and Derrida. Deconstruction, rather than destroying universal categories, illuminates their internal conflicts and tensions allowing what they fear and repress (the feminine, the other) to emerge. **Jacques Rancière** welcomes Derrida's explorations of democracy. Against the triumphalism of the ideologists who try to spread democracy to the world with tanks and fighter planes and against the sobriety of those who fear that too much democracy leads to bad policies and undermines government, Rancière argues that democracy is the only proper political form. Democracy's foundation is the absence of all foundations, its work carried out by the social part that has no part or visibility and fights in its particularity as representative of the universal. For **Drucilla Cornell**, Derrida's injunction is to assume the responsibility for creating new timelines, in which the future is always to come but always already part of our existence. For Cornell, our political responsibility is exemplified by Nelson Mandela's fidelity to a justice to come which, while lurking in the law, holds law's injustice to account. **Slavoj Žižek** in a wide-ranging essay reviews some key themes in his interpretation of Hegel and of Lacanian psychoanalysis in the context of recent attacks against critical theory. Despite differences with what he perceives as the ethical turn in deconstruction, he concludes that Derrida's *différance* expresses the same 'minimal difference' as his own concept of *parallax*. **J. Hillis Miller**, in a profoundly moving talk, discusses Derrida's late seminars. Through talking, writing, repetition, Derrida tried to defer death while, at the same time, incorporating it in his life. For Derrida, death has already come to the living, it is there from birth, life is lived posthumously and death is survived in the name. This is why Derrida was obsessed with ghosts and his revenant will keep coming back in myriad guises, texts and names, the communities-to-come in Derrida's name. **Costas Douzinas** celebrates a *bios eulogos* and *euéthés*. Derrida's name brings together life and oeuvre as blessing, the *arché* and *telos* of these communities of justice, still to come, in honour to the name. In **Ken McMullen's** film *Ghostdance*, shown as part of the series at the Lumière cinema, Derrida plays a French philosopher discussing the centrality of ghosts in film, philosophy and life. All the main themes of these eulogies are anticipated in Ken's film: the extended temporality of the future anterior, the performative and linguistic aspect of thinking, the immense kindness and generosity of Derrida the teacher, his ethical and political commitment. Watching Derrida, his ghost (in the film, he argues that cinema offers the most prominent ghosts of our times) discussing the many ghostly returns *avant le mort* was one of the most unsettling experiences of the series. Earlier versions of Gayatri Chakravorty Spivak and Drucilla Cornell's essays were published in *Differences* (16/3, 2006). A version of Slavoj Žižek's essay was published in *Critical Inquiry* (32/2, 2006).

Derrida always wrote for and with others. His texts are commentaries, treatises, occasionally footnotes on those of others. They are authentic and parasitic, original and copies at the same time: they enter, interrupt, disrupt and interlace themselves with the writings of others, from Plato, Kant, Rousseau, Hegel, Marx, Freud, Heidegger to Mallarmé, Joyce, Kafka, Celan, Bataille, Blanchot. Derrida's signature, singular and plural, unique in its iteration (he painstakingly explained the aporetic structure of the act of signing) was at the same time and always a counter-signature repeating, supplementing, annotating the first authorial signature. '[T]he only way to sign with a name-to-come is, or should be, a counter-signature', he wrote, 'counter-signing with the names of the others, or being true to the name of the other...So when I read another...the feeling of duty which I feel in myself is that I have to be true to the other; that is to counter-sign with my own name, but is a way that should be true to the other.' In this epistemology that reminds us Alain Badiou's, truth is the sense of fidelity to (the text of) the other; to be true is 'to add something, to give something to the other, but something that the other could receive and could, in his or her turn, actually or as a ghost countersign'.[5]

For Judith Butler, Derrida's 'writing constitutes an act of mourning, one that he is perhaps, *avant la lettre*, recommending to us a way to begin to mourn this thinker who not only taught us how to read, but gave the act of reading a new significance and a new promise'.[6] These essays take up this invitation, responding to Derrida's call to be faithful to the other. They are attempts to be faithful to Derrida, offerings to him, inviting him to countersign. Attending a conference on his work at the University of Luton, Derrida said that, listening to all the learned papers on 'Applying Derrida', he felt *as if* he were dead. We fear death, he wrote, because this will be the end of our world, the end of *the* world. But even scarier is the 'fantasy that we are going to be present at and in attendance at this non-world, at our death' not unlike the experience he had following all those papers discussing him, as if he was not there or as if he were dead.[7] Derrida was present at the Birkbeck lecture series. But strangely, for all of us, for the thousands of people who attended the lectures, Derrida was present not as if he were dead but as if he were alive. His (ghostly) presence haunts this volume as it will haunt many volumes, texts and generations to come.

***

What is Derrida's eulogy? Derrida's *eulogia* and the eulogy addressed to him? What is a *eulogy*?

1. *Eulogia: eu legein* or *kalos logos*, good words and speaking well, a good and fair speech or writing.
2. *Eulogia: bene-dictio* and benediction, a blessing; in particular, the blessing of baptismal rites.
3. Eulogy: speech or writing in praise of a person, especially someone who has died, funeral oration.
4. *Eu-logos:* (s)he who speaks well and beautifully; the *rhetor*, the poet, the speaker or writer of good and beautiful words. A person with good *logos*; someone with reason, the reason of the reasonable and of reasoning well; but also someone who is more than reasonable and reasoning well, a person who inhabits the beauty and goodness of reason, in good reason.

Which bond links the *eu-* of the beautiful and the good, the *logos* of language and reason and the eulogy of elegy or encomium? They all pass through the name. St John's baptismal ablutions and Pericles' funeral oration echo in the *eu-phonon* and *eu-morphon* of the *eu-logia*, in the clear sound, the beautiful rhythms and elegant schemes of the *eu-logos*. The *eulogia* of baptism or of circumcision is the second or symbolic birth, the eulogy of the funeral oration, the second or symbolic death. Baptism's nomination is literally an *onomatopoeia*:

onoma's poiesis, the making of a name and making through the name. The baptismal blessing is the *arché*, the beginning and the foundation. It bestows a proper name – Jacques, Jean-Luc, Drucilla – and this proper name will improperly provide a singular foundation and support throughout life's itinerary. The funeral eulogy, at the *telos*, the end and destiny, returns the name to the other, confines it to memory and mourning. A benediction, a blessing and speaking well, brings us to life by creating the nominal support of identity, another takes it back. The infant acquires self through the *eulogia* of baptism and then surrenders it at the eulogy, the funeral oration. Life's itinerary will have been travelled in the interstices, the gap between the two eulogies, between the giving of name by the other (language, ritual, the father) and its abandonment to the safekeeping of others.

What is in a name? What is there in the proper name? A name is always proper, my property and propriety, what endows me with recognition and singularity. The proper name is the linguistic companion of unrepeatable identity, the mark of uniqueness, the linguistic equivalent of the face. And yet the *eulogia* that gives name and creates the unique self, blessing's performance, inscribes, at the same time, otherness in the midst of self. Hegel reminds us that language in its arbitrary connections between signifier and signified and between words and things destroys, kills reality. 'Say the word lion and you create the lion *ex nihilo*, by abolishing the tangible thing.'[8] 'Say the word dog and you kill the real dog...the conceptual understanding of empirical reality is equivalent to a murder' agrees Kojéve.[9] Say the word 'elephants' adds Lacan and here comes a herd of elephants, present in its absence and filling up the room. The word nihilates the thing, brackets the body but creates the subject, whose unity is constructed by signifiers, the proper name. This is the meaning of Lacan's infamous statements that the 'signifier represents a subject...(not a signified) – for another signifier (which means not for another subject)'[10] or, that 'language before signifying something signifies for someone'.[11] The subject speaks and comes to existence by being spoken in language, by being alienated from bodily and sensory experience into the cold world of the sign. The name comes from the other, it is always the name of another. Self is the result of a nomination and a nominalism: I exist because I have been addressed by the (m)other, in the other's idiom, in a first foundational family naming; l exist because language has given me name.

Baptism's giving of name is the performative *par excellence*. But the given name is never fully proper, never completely ours. Our name is the effect of linguistic and legal manoeuvres (of a felicitous speech act), of the operation of the legal rules and religious blessings, public rituals and family conventions, which regulate the baptismal onomatopoeia and determine its effects. The named self is a gift of language, the construct of law and convention. My name, my mark of uniqueness, has been imported from outside, my most proper is a gift, blessing or curse placed on me. As the Medievals said, the name determines destiny, the *fatum* is *fata*, the *nomen omen*. A bad name is half the road to Hell. Our name comes from the place of the other, the name the father bestows, the name of the father. But it also comes from the place of the law, institution, religion and all the other conventions that determine right and wrong. Our name, our most proper, is right from the start an imposition. It makes Derrida out of 'Derrida' but also keeps the two separate and places the other (the father and the big Other) in the midst of self. '[W]hen I say I am Applied Derrida,' said Derrida at a conference called 'Applied Derrida' 'this means that, from the very beginning, I received this name, this name was imprinted on me…I was applied Derrida when I received the seal of the name from the family and much more than the family. It was applied to my body in a way which was not simply literal and physical…I was and I am still Applied Derrida, with, at the same time, a feeling of passively suffering this application having a feeling of having a duty to the name…I love this name which is not mine of course.'[12]

My name is not mine. It is applied on/to me, I am the application and repetition of a word. This is how the structure of iterability and the misadventures of the signature start. I am unique in being called a name, in listening to my name, those two arbitrary syllables, as if it was another's, in responding to its call and being responsible for it. The initial nomination and the constitutive *eulogia* (your name is Co-stas) is repeated in every calling and interpellation, every 'Hey, you' which creates the 'me' answering the 'you', my name reiterating the blessing and the rules and conventions it carries and confirms. The singularity I am is an effect of the repeated operation of nomination's blessing.

A mark that becomes singular through repetition, this is what makes identity plural. Discussing Martin Heidegger's attempt to present Nietzsche's writings as a grand totality of meaning, Derrida explores the strategies used to give coherence, completeness and consistency to the work of an author. The name is the most important: 'Nietzsche – the name of the thinker here – names the cause of his thinking.'[13] The name stands for the totality of a life or represents the wholeness of a subject matter or an *oeuvre*. For Heidegger, the whole of western metaphysics could be gathered under the single name of Nietzsche. Derrida accepts the constitutive role of nomination, baptism's onomatopoeia but immediately deconstructs it. 'But whoever has said that a person bears a single name?'[14] Nietzsche kept multiplying his names and signatures, his identities and masks. 'My name is legion' Nietzsche would say.

The *onomatopoeia* of baptism brings self to life as an effect of otherness. The other is part of self right from the start, every time we answer our name, we respond in our name but at the same time in the name of the other. *Je es un autre*, as Rimbaud memorably put it. The name splits self straight from the start into a legion of parts and shards, roles and identities, the masks and *personas* the name imposes and allows us to wear. If metaphysics 'has constantly repeated and assumed that to think and to say must mean to think and say something that would be as one, one matter',[15] the *eulogia* of baptism opens the multi-fold. The name disseminates and is disseminated, it spreads out its effects, in a multiplicity of lives and deaths. But in each signature, each call, each honour addressed to it, the name anticipates its proper coming in death. 'The name alone makes possible the plurality of deaths.'[16]

If the *eulogia* of baptism creates by multiplying, displacing, disseminating, the eulogy of the funeral oration gathers, condenses, simplifies. The eulogy mirrors *eulogia*. Eulogia's temporality is the future anterior: the proper name is always in the future, more accurately, the proper name will have been in the future, it will have been completed in the funeral oration, in the second symbolic death. The good words, the good reasons of the *eulogos* will have confined the name *in memoriam*, in the recollection of mourning and memory. It is in this sense, that my name is never fully mine; answering my name, signing in my name anticipates the point when I and my name will have been gathered together by others, in memory. My time, my life will have been a delay, a deferment, the ecstases of temporality opened by the future eulogy, when 'my' name as memory will singularly inhabit the other (no longer me, I will no longer *be*). The future eulogy opens the possibilities within which the name unfolds its past and present.

The possibility of invoking the name in a eulogy or funeral oration, of remembering, through speaking well, him who was always dismembered (in books, articles, films, interviews), indicate the structure of naming from the start, from the second symbolic birth of nomination. The name predicts and acts out the death of the named; the nomination of baptismal rites both brings the person to life and splits it, as part of its necessary possibility. 'In calling or naming someone while he is alive, we know that his name can survive him and already survives him; the name begins during his life to get along without him, speaking and bearing his death each time it is pronounced in naming or calling each time it is inscribed in a list, or a civil registry, or a signature.'[17] The name bestows uniqueness and singularity but also predicts and pre-figures death, every baptismal blessing and nomination preparing the funeral oration, the point at which the name will be just a name, abandoned to the circulation of language without referential support and to the interiority of memory without answer and recourse.

At the moment of death, the name survives. When I offer a eulogy to Derrida, I who met him a few times but did not know *him*, in the sense of being a personal friend, I address 'Derrida', a huge thesaurus of texts, stories, lectures, occasional encounters, an immense body of work, work without a body. 'Derrida' is a huge world, an ecumene and cosmopolis but also an intimate part of my own world, my thoughts, memories, emotions and acts. In this sense, I am like the grave or the funereal urn, I carry in me the name of him who is no longer there: the name of the dead is cinders. Derrida can no longer answer when we call him, he can no longer say 'here I am'; but we know, think and speak to 'Derrida', well and beautifully, offer eulogies, elegies and encomia to the memory of Derrida or to 'Derrida'.

The necessary dislocation between the person with his name(s)-always-to-come and the textual archive bearing the name, between Derrida and 'Derrida' is the work of death: 'it is as if death cut the name off in the midst of life, severed the name from the living one who bore it, and this would be precisely its work as death, the operation proper to it; as if death separated the name and the body, as if it tore the name away from the body...'.[18] Death removes the named from the name, the referent from the sign, splits spirit and letter. This departure and separation marks the entombment and confinement of the dead in the body of the other (the symptom of mourning), the final entrustment of the name to the other's reminiscence (the effect of memorisation). At this moment, finally, the name becomes proper, it comes to its own. The dead is re-membered in the re-collection of his name. Mourning, the committal of the name to the crypt of the other's remembrance. The *eulogia* will have made the eulogy possible. Baptism, a naming-towards-eulogy.

But the separation and splitting of body and name, of spirit and letter has been there all along, from the blessing of baptism and circumcision. It has been active before death and pre-figuring death. Every time I read a 'Derrida', I severed the living person from its name, every time I referred, quoted or mentioned 'Derrida', I separated the body from the *anima* of the *onoma*. The baptismal *eulogia* endows us with the property of a name, gives us the identity of the signifier. We know well, all too well today, how the signifier is caught in the ambiguities and uncertainties of the signifying chain, always deferred and differing, even when (mainly when) it arrives. This breaking of anchor, this sliding of the name, which can never match our 'real' selves, always dependent on and in relationship with the other (the other signifier, the other in me) encrypts and encodes death in each. The name identifies by misrepresenting, ascribes (mistaken) recognition, predicts and acts out the work death will complete 'all the time, especially when we speak, write and publish'.[19]

The name has been separated from the body, the corpus from the corpse, threnody the eulogists. 'This is the case when others use or speak our name, either before or after our death, but also when we ourselves use our name.'[20] The name is always in advance of its memory; name and memory cannot be separated. Death reveals that a name can always give itself to repetition in the absence of its bearer, becoming a singular common noun, like the pronoun 'I' which effaces singularity as it designates it; the *I*, before the verb is the most common exteriority but it marks, at the same time, the greatest interiority, self's relationship to itself. Memory's name too 'preserves an essential and necessary relation with the possibility of the name, and of what in the name assures preservation'.[21] The power of the name is to allow us to keep calling the named although he is not there to answer, although he can no longer answer in his name. Death shows the power of the name. This is the name of personal memory of the *mnémé* of thoughts, ideas, texts, readings. We are now responsible for the name, witnesses to its honour.

The addressee of the eulogy is not there, he is absent, dead. And yet, it is him, Derrida, that the eulogy addresses. The dead 'is here and he is not here, in his name and beyond his name'.[22] The eulogy, the second symbolic death, is the recognition that he is not here, that he will never be here again. This is the necessary recognition of the death of the friend and of death itself – and this recognition creates community. And yet, the dead is also there, if only in name and in memory. The same eulogy that announces the *telos* of the friend and consigns him to memory, returns the dead to the honour of the name, makes Derrida 'Derrida' forever. Absence of the addressee, presence of the name. But it is not only the addressee who is not present. For a eulogy to work, for it to be *eumorphos*, *eurythmos* and *euschemos*, it must remove, as much as possible (it is never fully possible), the authority of the speaker, his narcissism and *amour propre*. Otherwise, it becomes self-serving and hypocritical, an attempt to prove the superiority of the orator, his emotions, memories, ideas. Speaker and addressee are both absent in the funeral oration, as they congregate and converge around the name, in an *Adieu Derrida*. Absence of the writer, absence of the reader: as Derrida taught us these are the structural characteristics of writing. All writing mimics the eulogy, it predicts, foreshadows and acts out the death of its author. 'Readability bears this mourning: a phrase can be readable, it must be able to become readable, up to a certain point, without the reader, he or she, or any other place of reading, occupying the ultimate position of addressee. This mourning provides the first chance and terrible condition of all reading.'[23] Writing and reading have the characteristics of a funeral oration, the reader caught in the gap between the name and the text.

In an exchange which did not lead to a contractual agreement, in a reciprocation and recognition of the other in the same, Jacques Derrida and Jean-Luc Nancy addressed the *adieu* that one says before the other, before the dead other. Derrida's many eulogies for dead friends had been translated into English and published in an American edition, later 'translated back' and published in France. In a short introduction to the French edition entitled *Chaque fois unique, la fin du monde* Derrida mentioned Jean-Luc Nancy's *Noli me tangere*[24] and called the 'adieu', a salute we address to a dead friend. Every time a friend dies, each unique death does not announce solely absence or disappearance, but the end of the whole world, of all possible world, and 'each time the end of world as unique totality, irreplaceable and infinite'.[25] Death is the singular and irreversible end of the world, both for the dead other but also for the 'provisional survivor', who endures this impossible experience, an experience of this no-thing, this nothing that is death, an experience we will never have as such but only under sufferance, before the death of the other. A world, each world, is unique and irreplaceable, singular and infinite, and the death of the other gives it its full meaning.

This is the theme that Jean-Luc Nancy takes up in his 'Consolation, desolation' an immediate short reaction to Derrida's death, which becomes a much longer contemplation on Derrida's world in the present volume. Death carries in it the whole world because all world is unique and integral. The friend's salute, his eulogy, is a blessing, it touches the untouchable. Saying 'adieu Derrida' calls the other by his name, calls his name, keeps the other (name) in me. The eulogy salutes the other 'in the untouchable integrity of his insignificant property, his name already plunged in the non-significance of the proper name and through him or in him, every time, of the world in its totality'.[26] If Derrida no longer responds, it is because he is responding in us, 'in us right before us, – in calling us, in recalling to us: a-Dieu'.[27]

Is the 'Adieu', the 'farewell', community's salute, a *bienvenu* and welcome to communion? Does death incorporate the dead into community? A community of religion or nation, of people or ideology? Does death complete what has been inchoate, does it give meaning to what is shared? The death of the other is always singular, it cannot be shared, it is only his or hers, never mine. The other does not live and will not return. Death has no meaning for the dead nor can it be shared by the survivors. Only my death is fully mine but I will not experience it either. And yet, because I will not experience death, it is only through the death of the other that I come to a reckoning of death. 'If death is indeed the possibility of the impossible...then, man, or man as Dasein, never has a relation to death as such, but only to perishing to demising, and to the death of the other...The death of the other thus becomes..."first", always first.'[28] This is the role of the eulogy, of the second death: to salute the dead other who is always 'first' and to salute death itself before its time, on the way.

The dead Derrida does not live in himself; he lives now in us, who call his name and write to him and for him.

> This being 'in us', the being 'in us' of the other, in bereaved memory, can be neither the so-called resurrection of the other *himself* (the other is dead and nothing can save him from this death, nor can anyone save us from it), nor the simple illusion of a narcissistic fantasy in a subjectivity that is closed upon itself or even identical to itself... Already installed in the narcissistic struc-ture, the other so marks the self of the relationship to self, so con-ditions it that the being 'in us' of bereaved memory becomes the *coming* of the other... the first coming of the other.[29]

This other in the midst of self, this other who both constitutes and dislocates selfhood has been there from the start, from the *eulogia* of baptism, even if we may recognise it only at the moment of the second death. 'For even before the unqualifiable event called death, interiority (of the other in me, in you, in us) had already begun its work. With the first nomination, it preceded death as another death would have done.'[30]

It is this relationship to the (dead) other in me and in the other and, to death, that gives rise to community. Death cannot be sepa-rated from community but not in the sense of death being commu-nity's truth. No, the death of the other does not confirm or close community. Everything we say to the friend remains in us or between us, in the living who are left with his name and memory. What we say to him is the recognition of his death and of death, the recogni-tion of finitude. His world has come to an end, it is the end of the world but at the same time my world and that of all others has changed. 'When I say Roland Barthes,' says Derrida addressing the dead friend, 'it is certainly him whom I name, him beyond his name. But since he himself is now inaccessible to this appellation, since this nomination cannot become a vocation, address, or apostrophe... it is him in me that I name, toward him in me, in you, in us that I pass through his name. What happens around him and is said about him remains between us. Mourning began at this point.'[31] His single name is the 'between us', what brings us together. We speak to each other, we speak to ourselves, as we address Derrida, eulogists of the name.

Such is the beginning of community. Not in the sense of laws, institutions, politics, of what we call a tradition or history. These are just surface manifestations of humanity's acknowledgment of its deathbound finitude. Created by memory or in memory, community is the being-with-the-other, the being-together with death. But as Derrida put it parenthetically in his eulogy for Jean-François Lyotard 'one is never *ensemble*, never together, in an *ensemble*, in a group, gathering, whole or set, for the ensemble, the whole, the totality that is named by this word, constituted the first destruction of what the adverb *ensemble* might mean: to be *ensemble*, it is absolutely necessary not to be gathered into any sort of *ensemble*.'³² This together that does not create club, party or people is the community Jean-Luc Nancy has called 'inoperable'. It takes place

> through others and for others...if community is revealed in the death of others, it is because death itself is the true community of *I*'s that are not egos...A community is the presentation to its members of their mortal truth...the presentation of the finitude and irredeemable excess that makes up finite being: its death, but also its birth, and only the community can present me my birth, and along with it the impossibility of reliving it, as well as the impossibility of my crossing over into my death.³³

In death, through his death, Derrida has called us to a community that is not empirical or ideal, individualistic or communitarian, national or international. This is a community created every time we call Derrida, we write or talk about 'Derrida', a community never fully here or now, not unlike the justice or the democracy or the International to come. It cannot be different, 'because it is, for many of us, impossible to write without relying on him, without thinking with and through him. "Jacques Derrida", then, as the name for the future of what we write.'³⁴

***

'Eulogia ara kai euarmostia kai euschémosuné kai euruthmia euétheiai akolouthei, ouch hén anoian ousan hupokorizomenoi kaloumen [hôs euétheian], alla tén hôs aléthôs eu te kai kalôs to éthos kateskeuas-menén dianoian.' [Good, beautiful words and harmony, beauty of

form and of rhythm all follow from good ethos; and I don't mean that lack of thought and care for the world which we hypocritically call 'goodness' but the ethos that shapes a mind in truth and beauty.][35]

This is how Plato describes in the *Republic* the aims of education and culture and the perfection of character. Plato writes that *eulogia*, good and beautiful logos, harmony, form and rhythm are the gifts of the good ethos, the openness to the world. This is Derrida's eulogy, his good word and our word to him: he brought together reason and beauty, philosophy and literature, justice and law, ethos and the world. His words were a blessing, his name and memory our own *eulogia*. We can predict with confidence that centuries of readings will set the name 'Derrida' as their *arché*, enigma and *telos*. In writing to Derrida, or on 'Derrida', in writing some of the numberless texts that will address him (himself in myself and in all the others in the community of the Derrida-to-come), we give to him something that he would have hopefully accepted, we ask him to counter-sign our meagre eulogy, in truth, which is fidelity to the other, to the other in me, in truth, to the name of the dead other.

Derrida's life and work has been a long commentary on this passage of the *Republic*. In the same way, Plato's encomium to *eulogia* had already anticipated Derrida's eulogy. Adieu Derrida.

Notes

1. Jacques Derrida, *Adieu to Emmanuel Levinas* (Pascale-Anne Brault and Michale Naas, trans.) (Stanford: Stanford University Press, 1999) 9.
2. Frances Stonor Saunders, 'What have Intellectuals ever Done for the World?' *Observer*, 28 November 2004, 29.
3. The lectures were delivered in the following order: Jean-Luc Nancy, J. Hillis Miller, Gayatri Chakravorty Spivak, Slavoj Žižek, Etienne Balibar, Alain Badiou, Drucilla Cornell.
4. See the excellent Editors' Introduction in Jacques Derrida, *The Work of Mourning* (Pascale-Anne Brault and Michael Naas, eds) (Chicago: University of Chicago Press, 2001) 1–30. This book, which was an inspiration when we planned this lecture series, collects a number of eulogies delivered by Derrida.
5. Jacques Derrida, 'As if I were Dead' in J. Brannigan et al. (eds), *Applying: To Derrida* (London: Macmillan Press, 1996) 219.

6. Judith Butler, 'Jacques Derrida', *London Review of Books*, 4 November 2004, 32.
7. Derrida op. cit., n. 5, 215, 216.
8. *Hegel and the Human Spirit: a Translation of the Jena Lectures on the Philosophy of the Spirit (1805–6) with Commentary* (L. Rauch, trans.) (Detroit: Wayne State University Press, 1983) 89–95.
9. Alexandre Kojéve, Introduction to the Reading of Hegel's *Phenomenology of Spirit* (A. H. Nichols, trans.) (Ithaca: Cornell University Press, 1989) 140–1.
10. Jacques Lacan, 'Radiophonie' 2/3 *Scilicet*, 1970, 65.
11. Jacques Lacan, *Ecrits* (Paris: Seuil, 1966) 82–3.
12. Derrida, op. cit., n. 5, 219.
13. Jacques Derrida, 'Interpreting Signatures (Nitetzsche/Heidegger): Two Questions' in D. Michelfeder and R. Palmer (eds) *Dialogue and Deconstruction* (New York: University of New York Press, 1989) 60.
14. Ibid., 67.
15. Ibid., 68.
16. Derrida, 'Roland Barthes' op. cit., n. 4, 46.
17. Jacques Derrida, *MEMOIRES for Paul de Man* (Cecile Lindsay, Jonathan Culler and Eduardo Cadava, trans.) (New York: Columbia University Press) 49.
18. Derrida, 'Sarah Kofman' op. cit., n. 4, 178–9.
19. Ibid., 179.
20. Pascale-Anne Brault and Michale Naas, 'To Reckon with the Dead: Jacques Derrida's Politics of Mourning', Editors Introduction, op. cit., n. 4, 14.
21. Derrida, op. cit., n. 17, 49.
22. Derrida, 'Jean-François Lyotard', op. cit., n. 4, 226.
23. Ibid., 220.
24. Jean-Luc Nancy's *Noli me tangere* (Paris: Bayard, 2003).
25. 'Avant Propos', in Pascale-Anne Brault and Michael Naas (eds) *Chaque fois unique, la fin du monde* (Paris: Galilee, 2003) 9.
26. Jean-Luc Nancy, 'La Déclosion Consolation, Desolation' in *La Déclosion* (Paris: Éditions Galilée, 2005).
27. Jacques Derrida, op. cit., n.d., 13.
28. Jacques Derrida, *Aporias: Dying* (Thomas Dutoit, trans) (Stanford: Stanford University Press, 1994) 75.
29. Derrida op. cit., n. 17, 21–2.
30. Derrida, 'Roland Barthes' op. cit., n. 4, 46.
31. Ibid.
32. Derrida, 'Jean-François Lyotard', op. cit., n. 4, 225.
33. Jean-Luc Nancy, *The Inoperative Community* (Minneapolis: University of Minnesota Press, 1991) 14–5.
34. Butler op. cit., n. 6.
35. Plato, *Republic* book 3, (7.79), page 400.

2
Mad Derrida: *Ipso facto cogitans ac demens*

Jean-Luc Nancy

'It's absolutely mad'

Michel Foucault and Jacques Derrida put into play, in a famous debate, not only two ways of reading Descartes, but also two ways of interpreting the alleged division that the pair of terms 'reason' and 'madness' presuppose. We will not recall here the precise terms of that debate. Let me just recall that whereas Foucault identified the exclusion of unreason in the institution of classical rationality, Derrida replied by arguing that the so-called subject of the so-called reason could not be determined, identified or presented without his or her subjectivity [*subjectité*] being *ipso facto* ascribed under both headings of 'madness' and 'reason'.

Ipso facto: this expression means 'by the fact itself' [thereby], alternatively 'by the sameness of the fact', and was sometimes replaced by *eo ipso*, 'by that very act (or quality)' or imperceptibly, in Latin, 'through that alone', if not, more meticulously 'through that alone itself' [*de lui lui même*] [OED]; this expression is used here precisely to mean the 'same' and the sameness of the same. What is at stake here is the cardinal statement *ego sum*, which is far from signifying simply 'I am', since it announces the subject of the *sum* – the first person singular already *thereby* inscribed (*eo ipso*) in the verbal form *sum* without the need of an additional pronoun – the subject of that 'being' declared by the verb, that being itself in its most proper ontological quality (in its very *being*), that being or beings [*étant*] in so far as it is. *I* am it, me who states it, *ego*, in fact a superfluous pronoun,

17

whose excessive character turns out to be co-extensive and co-essential with the ontological property at stake.

***

Let us pause here for a moment in order to clarify our premise: we are not interested in the debate itsel.f between the two authors. We will take for granted two simple propositions:

1) Foucault and Derrida operated on different levels. Foucault was interested in the history of the practical and theoretical schemes of 'reason', of the representations and operations carried out under their guidance (the 'containment' of madness). Derrida, on the other hand, was concerned with the philosophical operation – whatever shape its epochal configuration takes – in so far as it cannot do less than endeavour to keep in suspense, indeed to thwart the schemes and representations of reason at its disposal, at any point in time [*dans le cadre de son temps*]. In other words, Derrida was concerned with what, under the heading of philosophy (but no matter under which heading, the latter must also be kept suspended), can resist all forms of assignation or prior determination of what 'reason' means. In principle – which means that the principle here is to deny all principles, failing which the shortest first step would remain impossible. Derrida's deep-seated disposition could only be understood by the yardstick of Descartes himself: a general suspension of all assent; alternatively, in Hegelian terms, a radical and essential *skepsis* (doubt) at the heart of the philosophical act itself; or, in Husserlian terms, an *épaché*, which precludes the imposition or imputation of a consti-tuted meaning. In any case, it is impossible to identify 'philosophy' with any determinable kind of 'rationality'.

2) There is a paradox in this debate. Foucault, who first of all pre-sented himself in sympathy, indeed empathy, with the 'madness' the rationalist apparatus tries to repress and constrain and whose work indeed provides many remarkable examples of that proximity or intimacy with the uncanny character of madness; Foucault, who sensed so well how madness suspends the possibility of the work, in other words, the possibility of the cathartic or apotropaic *poiesis* elaborated by the unbearable encounter with the non-face; Foucault remained marooned on the shores of reason, caught up in its dis-courses and works. This was the only space from which the concep-

tual, medical, social and institutional closure, the culture of which he was describing so well, could be identified. Playing on the opposite side, Derrida was, at least implicitly, committing himself not to let this closure simply close *in front* of him or his discourse, but to let, on the contrary, in some way and at some point, the trace of the closure to be blurred, torn or opened, thus running the risk and taking the chance of throwing reason into a panic instead of grounding madness.

Let us begin again, after these remarks which, we should make clear, did not aim to validate or endorse one position by invalidating the other. Rather, they point to an irreducible heterogeneity, which is present whenever philosophy endeavours to be itself.

To come to the same (thing)

To say philosophy 'itself' – is precisely to utter a difficulty, an uneasiness [*inquiétude*], indeed an anxiety and an aporia about the identification of philosophy *itself* (properly itself, without uncertainty, identical to itself). Philosophical reason – the *sophia* itself, then, or the *logos*, *pure* reason, Spirit or the Will, Intuition or Thought. All these terms gravitate, more or less favourably, heavily, around an identical and immutable centre of gravity, if not in the immediate vicinity of a black hole. *Philosophical reason does not come to the same (thing)*: not to the same as some other reason which one would be able to find or to invoke, not even to the same as a reason which could exclude madness, and thus it never either comes to the same as itself.

This is what Derrida ceaselessly explored and what made him oppose that more intimate dissension in reason 'itself' to Foucault's sharing between reason and its other. This is why he had to embrace that madness within which reason sinks *ea ipsa* when it succeeds in identifying itself – unless the reverse be true, which is to say, unless Derrida came to philosophy, destined for it in a frenzied manner, driven by a madness. As we know, Derrida displayed his intimacy with frenzy [*forcené*], as with other figures of strayed furore [*fureur égarée*]. (This does not mean that Foucault was not driven, in fact, by another and similar madness. If I am allowed to give a simplistic account, however, the contrast between them was that between a thought devoted to warding off its madness and another warding off its reason. Let it be clear, however, that we are not psychologising here; rather we are presenting at most a characteriology of thought.)

Contrary to what unthinking commentators or hasty interpreters have been claiming, Derrida never conspired against the *subject*. Rather, he recognised in it the necessary crossing of identity and difference (of identity and *its* difference). If he never practically thematised or problematised that crossing under the heading of the 'subject', it is precisely because, from the outset, that term seemed overdetermined, either by the vacuity of the Kantian unity which appropriates representations, or, on the contrary, by the blocking of the completeness of the ego. In either case, the premise itself was under suspicion: that the subject is a substratum or a *suppositum* [*suppôt*] of the self, essentially able to support and to relate self to itself (to the same), a substance without accident. Despite this, Derrida never gave up the affirmation of the first person, therefore nor of the *person* itself, even if that term is not part of his vocabulary for the obvious reason that it is compromised with the hypocritical smugness of the 'human person' (with its life, dignity and a concise handbook of rights).

Philosophy has rarely, probably never, known of the first person, of a philosophical writing written in the first person since Nietzsche, Kierkegaard and Descartes (or else, since Plato's dialogical *mimesis* – we should indeed pay attention to all the dialogues in Derrida, to all the 'you', in the singular and the plural, at which the 'I' is directed – dispatched, entrusted to, devoted to, alienated – unless it is, more obscurely, since the 'I engender time' of the Kantian schematism, or of the Heideggerian *Jemeinigkeit*). But Derrida makes exceptional use of an utterance and a personal perforation, an egological punching out of the concept, indeed, an exorbitant or extravagant, in a nutshell, mad use, when he claims to depart from the reasonable and regular anonymity of reason.

There is a simple question which has been neglected so far. Why has Derrida written so much in the first person and in conformity with all the roles of that person, such as the transcendendal *ego*, the character in a dialogue, the signatory, the one who confesses, the dispatcher of cards and letters? Its importance lies in the way it performs madness in reason and the madness of reason, as much as it perforates reason with madness, with its own madness. The first person both challenges the impersonality of the discourse of reason and pretends to substitute itself for it, carrying out alone – *ea ipsa* – the performance or the performing [*performation*] of a truth *seipsam patefaciens* at the same time as it perforates that patefaction of the only singular opening of its elocution.

***

As for the manifest abuse of assonances and of all kinds of verbal contacts, contractions and contaminations, that alliterative outburst which, by the way, I just imitated, let us decide its fate. Yes, it is Derrida's madness to make an alliteration resound indefinitely, an alliteration in which he wants to hear and make us hear – and *be* heard – not only the literal or literary assonance counter-posed to the tonelessness [*détimbrage*] and the flatness [*matité*] of the pure concept, but also the allotropic iteration of which the subject cannot but be seized, and of which we will now speak. It is certainly a dangerous madness, on the brink of a hyperbolic cratylism – as if the word '*différance*' or '*destinerrance*' had to give form to the thing itself. However, the latter also foils itself or in any case defies itself (and distrusts itself) by pretending not to constitute 'a word, or a concept', by multiplying frenetically its linguistic, stylistic and bookish effects all the more to abandon them, disseminated, like pebbles carried away by its raging flow. If Foucault's madness is the absence of a work, that of Derrida is the excess of a work, a double polarity.

***

Writing (saying, letting out, throwing) *I*, Derrida shows, as anyone who uses that word, that the one who says/writes 'I' instantly detaches and leaves outside of himself or herself that operator of identity. That deposition or exposition maddens as much as it assures. It maddens him in order to assure him, and precisely because it assures him.

In the enunciative ontology of the *ego sum*, Descartes recognises above all that the *logos* here is not *about* being [*au sujet de l'être*] but, rather, it is *the subject of* being and the essence of a substance whose whole quality is to relate to itself. Descartes knew that and took care

to specify that the validity of the *egological* truth is co-extensive with
its pronouncement. The ego subsists by saying itself and *by the very
fact* of its saying: *eo ipso, ego*. It comes into the world in so far as it is
staged and put into play through its utterance – and therefore, in so
far as the irreducible gap between self, as the subject of its enunciation, and itself, as the subject of its utterance, appears suddenly, as a
gap that no science of linguistics can reduce and no poem can fill in.
This gap determines the coming into the world as a staging (he will
be the actor of his own role) and as a gambling (with the gain of the
subject and the loss of the substance, or else the reverse: henceforth
the *logo-* and the *onto-* play against each other in the two senses of
'against'). A theatre of errors, a tragi-comic illusion.

Descartes specifies that the utterance – *ego sum* – may be verbal or
mental. This equivalence introduces, surreptitiously, if not an aggra-
vation, at least a severe confirmation of the harsh laws of egology. If
the *mens* is equivalent to the *vox* (while the *vox*, at this textual
moment of the *Second Meditation*, is equivalent to its *scriptum*, to its
left trace, exposed and deferred in itself, as the Husserlian instant of
the living present is), it is because the voice *calls itself* as much as the
writing *remembers* [*se rappelle*]. It resonates, it resounds in order to be,
and in order to resound it must have a hollow body. Why would
Descartes' and Derrida's body, or that of anyone who says 'I', not be
the same as these glass bodies with which the madmen imagine
themselves endowed, according to Descartes? How could that body
not tremble when resounding with its own call? What it utters – *sum*,
I am – calls it away, very far away; *ego* as an echo which hardly comes
back to itself, which comes back to itself only by breaking and losing
itself, and which nevertheless returns to itself [*se revient*] and remembers from the most immemorial, the most ante-predicative, the most
pre-natal and insane place. *Mens seipsam dementat*: the spirit maddens
itself at the very moment it spiritualises itself.

Where the subject gets lost

Derrida appears to me – with Artaud so close to him as to be able to
touch him despite the different *frenzies* – as someone who has had
one day, and probably every time he speaks and thinks, the experience of that dementia which constitutes the most remarkable and
the most terrible present modern man has managed to give himself:

the coincidence with oneself takes place through a collision whereby the substance and the subject break against each other. The accident becomes essential.

From the moment that thinking comes down to experiencing itself thinking (is this not the case since Parmenides and Plato or Augustine and Anselm?) it also experiences the meaninglessness of something for which a relation is impossible because it is the relation itself. This is the quality of the *ego* as *ego ipse*, the *ipso facto* of the ego, recognised as stemming from a fact of language and from the fugitive consignation of a trace which will never lead us back to that of which it is the trace.

He is maddened (Derrida, the subject) to find nothing but his trace and to find this trace fading away. He is maddened to find that he is a trace [*de se trouver trace*]. He must redraw himself [*se retracer*] – picture himself again – so as to attempt to retain a little of what he knows absolutely that he is not able to retain, even though he can touch it, but always only touch it, without seeing or knowing it, without possessing or understanding it, not even being able to want to possess or understand it at the risk of willing to possess willing itself, and its furious rage.

Derrida deploys as a result the power of the enunciative ontology, in an insatiable, unrelenting uttering, following the most archaic decision. Always prevent the echoing speech of the *ego* from stopping to resound, the echoing speech of the *ego*, which can only compose itself alliteratively in order to come close to the very small amount of reason its madness lets shine, during the incalculable time of the coincidence *eo ipso*, a coincidence which is impossible and certain, fortuitous, eternal, contingent and necessary, luminous and mortal, hopeless.

This very small amount of reason, whereby reason faints when assuring itself about itself [*s'assurant de soi*], maddening itself through that very assurance, stems from nothing less than the other in self, which self recognises – the other, itself, its language, its gender, its friend, its law, its voice, its trace – as constituting the heart of Kantian freedom, of the Hegelian spirit, of the Heideggerian being, finally, of the Cartesian *ego* which makes itself here more faultlessly, more madly known at the vanishing point of an original loss. The nerve, the knot or the high point, the nerve-meter [*le pèse-nerfs*], which maddens thought emerges as the property of an original loss and through this loss, in it, the origin disappears in its own opening. It is another version of the original sin, which does not befall but consti- tutes the subject. It constitutes it as a sinner, which is to say, indebted to the saintliness, which founds its existence (but one can only ever owe to saintliness).

Derrida does not use this language, but that of an incurable grief. The melancholy of the lost other (of the lost other in me, of the other lost by me, the other than me and the other me, the other innocent saint) will not be sublated by mourning, will not be redeemed by sal- vation. That grief drives him mad, or rather, that grief is mad, it is madness itself. It is the *straying* of reason in itself – which makes its law, its structure, its history and finally its very reason (its *raison d'être*, its fully sufficient reason).

What is lost this way – the other, the same – is what we could legiti- mately call the brother or the sister of reason. Derrida challenges few motifs as vehemently as that of fraternity. Without taking up again the details of that *disputatio*, I would like simply to make the follow- ing remark: not only is the brother given through the death of the father (in accordance, in fact, with the Freudian legend), but he may also be given only as having himself disappeared, lost from an origi- nal loss. To invoke fraternity, then, does not summon a familial model (natural, pertaining to blood relations, indeed, masculine – I leave aside here the problem of gender). Rather, it is a matter of moving the family away to the realm of the impossible. To speak of the 'family' amounts to speaking of the impossible tying together the necessary and the contingent, nature and culture, the aporia of all thought modelled on the scheme of the origin (of generation, of the *genos*, of the genre, etc.). De facto, the family, fraternity, co- originarity (which is to say, the origin in itself, if no origin can be represented otherwise than as a common origin) are, and must remain the impossible, the intolerable, the very risk of suffocation in the substance – and no subject emerges otherwise than by getting out and 'leaving one's mother and one's brothers'.

We should finally ask what could a command, or prescription of the impossible mean – for example, the prescription of a moral and political 'fraternity'. I will not elaborate further on that topic here. I only wanted to note that Derrida's madness is perhaps nothing else than such a confrontation with or such an exposition to the neces- sity of the impossible. (We are all bound to the impossible. However, there are two ways in which one lets oneself be bound by it: one is tuned to the impossibility of the impossible, the other to its possibility. To separate [*départager*] the one from the other is not easy – it is not possible. However, the separation [*partage*] is the same as that which distributes reason and madness as the unity of the *same* subject.)

Contingency and coincidence

Despite all this, in fact, the subject announces and presents itself. In fact, it touches its other. It reaches, touches itself and, at that very moment, it not only escapes (not by standing aside the present moment, but by escaping *in* the present itself); rather this very touch is the cause of its flight. It would not flee from itself, had he not found itself. He would not make itself impossible [*s'impossibiliserait*], had it not come up against that possibility. By reaching itself, it also repels itself, it pushes away from itself that self which can only be close according to a law of proximity, which imposes the greatest distance the more it approaches itself and its neighbourhood, its bordering [*côtoiement*], its flowering.

The subject knows therefore to be itself in the implacable distance of its proximity. It knows itself not to be so, and it knows itself not to be itself. It is gripped, hindered by that *double bind*, which pulls and stretches it out in opposite directions, like a torture victim pulled by four horses towards the four points of the compass.

Its reason is lost on contact with itself. When it encounters tangency, that coincidental contingency, which is also the point of the subject (of birth, of presence, of taking off [*partance*]) it maddens itself at that point. That madness has nothing exorbitant about it, nothing excessive or immoderate: it is measured exactly against the unity and the certainty of the subject of reason. To say it with Kant's help, 'madness' does not mean here *Schwärmerei* (delirium, an unbridled representation, the ignorance of the limits of experience); it designates, on the contrary, the *Trieb* of the unconditioned, the drive, desire, the power of reason towards a 'principle of principles', beyond which nothing else can be expected from reason and nothing is missing from its sufficiency. The subject of reason is not what it ought to be unless it is engaged – and thus strayed – in that properly exorbitant drive. Nothing must escape its mastery; reason must be capable of putting under its sovereignty its most proper and most intimate disappropriation [*ranger sous sa souveraineté*].

In this sense, its madness is a paranoia, the madness of identity and of the unconditional surveillance of everything that could undermine its absolute exception: an unidentifiable identity, which cannot be brought back to unity but is disseminated in its principle and is, for this reason, arch-originary [*archi-principielle*], which is to say archaic, archaeological, and architectonic up to the point where the *arché* precedes itself indefinitely, irrepressibly, anarchically, impossibly.

This same madness is modulated, however, in a schizophrenic mode. Its essence is a redoubling, a repetition of itself in itself, precisely, where reason itself, in redoubling itself, interrupts itself, coming to itself when it leaves itself. The reason of reason, the foundation of the foundation, the sameness of the identical, the mutual antecedence of the utterance and the enunciation, *ego sum*, 'me, I am', proclaimed in the absence or in the original loss of any I. This madness is therefore, on the one hand, the madness of belonging to oneself: it is mad for itself, in the sense in which one says 'he is mad for his body' (in fact, it is also mad for its body to the extent that its soul is far more intimately intertwined with the body than any captain can be with his ship). On the other hand, it is the madness of belonging to oneself only as to an other, in the other, in the sense that the *other* has no essential *in*-itself, to which self can be introduced and find himself again.

The 'other' means the same engulfed, thrown into itself in the abyss of the *into*. The interiority, the 'internal sense', which has no strict sense and no final reason except for re-absorbing in itself the totality of the outside, without remainder, at least without other remainder than the very movement of incorporation and absorption, the interminable intussusception.

To swallow oneself is what self cannot do. It cannot digest itself, not totally. There is always one too many or a missing one, who prevents self from becoming one, from being someone, simply one or uniformly ordinary like anyone who appears to be one.

Self needs the other, but the other is missing. The other leaves self as soon as it reaches it, as soon as it has contact with its sameness. The other disappears from the outset, and abandons it to what he ends up calling 'the *cogito* of the farewell'. I am, it says, biding far well, in taking its leave – 'farewell! farewell!' *'ade, ade'*, *'winke, winke'*, he says, as a German child, as a divine child, would do, in throwing the dice of contingency, that insignificant sign, that *Wink* signal of the god towards the *Ereignis*, towards the appropriating event, which always moves away as distantly as and distancing itself from the other.

Coagitation

This is the heart of madness: the proper, the appropriation, the exappropriation of the proper. The *cogito* of the farewell to the proper: I am, and I am in so far as I think that proper being or, I think myself properly being. I think, which is to say that I am towards myself in an identical position to that I am towards the object of my thought. I am thinking myself. I erase all distinctions concerning the object, I reduce them to my most proper subjective distinction. I grasp myself by grasping my being; that would go without saying, *eo ipso*, if only my being and the being which thinks did not immediately amount to two, at that very moment when unity is simultaneously *ipso facto* dislocated. Goodbye, then, goodbye already to the same and to the other at a single stroke.

The old identity of being and thought – this identity that suits reason – is lost when it finds and moves away from itself, when it touches itself. If this identity were to succeed, either being would evaporate or thought would reel. Farewell to the one or to the other – and perhaps also to the two together, when the subject *comes up* [se pointe] as a pure real cogitating itself (*coagitatio*, frenetic agitation from and between self and oneself).

In fact, there are two possible identifications of being and thought. The first subsumes being under a presupposed thought, and it produces a manic, destructive, dissolving, totalitarian madness. The second, confers the weight and the thickness of being to thought, the proof of a non-deducible existence. A secret madness results from this, elated only by maintaining itself at the limit of the possible from where it keeps watching out for the necessary as much as for the impossible, for the improbable and the incalculable.

The certainty of the *ego sum* is not rationally founded, since it is its own reason. The Cartesian evidence is as much invisible to itself as is illuminating. There is no reason at the foundation [*pas de raison au fond*], or no foundation to reason. There is no shop-sign at the Inn, says Leibniz. One cannot recognise oneself there. *Ego* and *Sum* found each other or, we could say, they take from each other the possibility of their certainty. Far from supporting each other, they only hold together thanks to a nervous trembling, a kind of shared blackout or vertigo, which abandons both being and thought to the insane.

This is how Derrida understands Descartes, and this is, at the same time, why he understands him. The point of certainty, the point of presence to oneself, the point of *ego* (far more than the point of 'the ego') is a point of rupture, a constitutive collapse of the 'ground which would be entirely my own'. Farewell, he says, I have lost you, I have already lost you, you who is more intimate to me than my intimacy, you who is more internal [*interné*] than my interiority. My egoity, my *Ereignis*, my *Eigenschaft* (my own quality), my *Eigentumn* (my own good), my sameness or my alterity (it is all the same, if it is 'mine', each time mine) alienates me in principle and originally, an alienation that expropriates me at the point of my propriation.

My unshakeable certainty, faced with the extravagant claims of the sceptics, becomes certain because it is unprovable and improbable, undecidable. Each time my assertion poses this certainty, my enunciation shows its fault. It is nothing more than an open mouth, which shows its dark recesses and the spasm of its glottis: *gl, ss, qual, ponge, différance*...a mad language, a borborygmic concept, *cogito* in the tone of a toll [*glas*], a *patho-logy* understood as a chiasmus of two terms, a pending language, an illness of language, a passion in the guise of language, a pathetic enunciation, an obsidian logic.

***

This patho-logy begins in a narrative or in an argument, of which language alone is the subject – which is to say that it is both its author and theme. An idiotic and idiomatic automatism takes charge or makes up for the self-constitution of *ego*. If there is a 'cogito of the farewell', it is because the instantaneous loss (in fact a transcendental or existential loss) of oneself (of the same and of the other) is immediately modulated into a long, really interminable farewell. It modulates itself; it complains, it pours out, it sings, it vocalises itself, it exclaims or writes itself – interminable threnody of a *se*, an *ipse*, *an oneself* in itself engulfed in the other and telling itself *farewell*, as it also says *come* and *yes*, as it salutes itself in the other, as it speaks to the other, as it dispatches itself and sends itself to the other, as other. It looks as if what is at issue is to find itself again by losing itself – not however through a compensation for the loss, but through the incalculable, indeterminable, undecidable hollowing out of the loss itself, in such a way that the loss might be alone in keeping the secret of *oneself* in general. This is what his pathology recites, his madness to be calling always for more language and for more languages in order to attest to the same, unique, irremediable errance.

Self-love

This is an amorous madness. It loves itself and it wants to be loved by itself. In other words, it wants in itself (in itself as a wholly other oneself) the other from all others, the singular absolute, indeed the object of a cherishment, of a dilection, of a predilection and of an election which is itself singular, absolute and irreplaceable. By loving the other in oneself, the other of oneself, it may be crossing without filling in or reducing the infinite distance of the loss and of the farewell.

This primitive passion is self-love, according to Rousseau, whose confession is to know himself as even more unrelated to the world than he is present to himself, but in this way, all the more outside of himself, more intimately alienated than any other strangeness in the world might be able to reach. Love is nothing else than self-love at the precise moment it loses its very object. It is the love of this strangeness, which presents itself by uttering the singular word *ego*, which does not designate anyone else but the speaker himself or herself, each time different. From Augustine to Descartes, Rousseau, Nietzsche and Rimbaud, it has never been otherwise. Self-love knows itself by losing its object in the other, abandoning its object to the other subject, to the inexhaustible alterity of the subject. That infinite loss drives him mad – mad with pain and joy, unable to distinguish tears from laughter.

Thus he is alone. Has anyone ever been more lonely [*seul*] than in madness? Has anyone ever been more lonely than Augustine, Descartes, Rousseau, Nietzsche, Rimbaud and Artaud? More alone than someone who does not relate to any other but remains abandoned, engulfed in his impossible unity as he is in the evidence of his own death (the death which takes the same away)? Being alone is to be prey to a self-love without object, to a madness that comes to the fore of that void, opened by the mouth whence 'ego' comes out, without vis-à-vis or face-to-face, without face or surface. Only the interval, between self and oneself, between the same and the other, between you and me, who is another you. *Ego sum* wants to hear itself respond *you are* – but it cannot know if it, in fact, hears more than its own will.

He is alone, he is mad, but his loneliness is populated with all similar solitudes. All those similarly afflicted in forlornness, equals in their *ego*, all equally incommensurable to their being-oneself as they are incommensurable with respect to each other, in spite of their equality or because of it. All properly inappropriate to their very being, to their *sum*, to their *existo*.

All love is the election of the proper. It wants the proper of the proper, it wants its *Ereignis*; it wants to *enteignen* itself and to *zueignen* itself to its *Ereignis* – to alienate itself and to devote itself to its appropriation. In the most ecstatic and mad passion, which is more intimate than any interiority that is exalted and loses itself in the other. No thinking about love can ignore this, irrespective of the way it wants to modulate it – love of bodies or ideas, of knowledge or beauty, of God, of the neighbour [*prochain*], of what is distant [*lointain*], of oneself, of the other. In the end, there is no difference between oblational and concupiscent love (others would say: between love and desire). There is only the difference through which the proper moves away from itself in order to appropriate itself – infinite difference which Derrida punctuates with the insane marking of its 'différance': *différance* of the farewell, of the *cogito*, of being and thought – opening of their sameness.

Self-love is the proper of love in so far as the proper, by distinguishing itself and by infinitely entrenching itself, by withdrawing itself beyond any propriety and all possible appropriation has no other injunction except to lose itself in itself and outside of itself. (To be sure, let us say in passing that this analysis cannot endorse the opposition Rousseau wishes to establish between, on the one hand, a primitive and innocent self-love and, on the other, a self-love that comes in contact with others through the desire to distinguish oneself. This opposition replays that between the love of God and self-love.) This is because the others are always already there; the desire for distinction always already mingles the wickedness of self-love with that of others. What we call ethics is played out at the place of this *mêlée*.

Oneself lost in itself and lost in oneself – or else *ego sum, ego existo* understood in its most literal translation: me I am, I go out, I present myself outside and consequently I stray. I stray 'me': I expose it and I exile it outside of its residence [*demeure*], or rather outside in the proper inside of its residence (outside in the inside of Descartes' stove), according to the delay, the differential moratorium attached to every residence, where one only ever resides in the expectation of a last home, where there will be no question of residing and of remaining (as he anxiously noted and pointed out).

Already now, however, here and at this very moment, permanently and without staying *there*, love properly entertains, animates and agitates the desire and the taste for oneself, for belonging to oneself and thus, for going without waiting, immediately, without reservations or delays to what has no hold on anything with or without mediation. Love indeed entertains the desire to go to this alterity of the same and the sameness of the other, to that madness of reason; finally, to the errancy of the *principium rationis* in which reason alone knows itself, according to the exorbitant event of its unconditionality, of its infinite and unfounded invention, of its properly insane transcendence (what he likes to call its 'deconstruction': the impossibility of completing the edifice and to hand over its keys, as much as to close the work's accounts).

Mad love is the proper of the proper who says farewell to oneself in itself and for itself, to the same in the other, therefore, also to the other as an other same. Derrida writes: 'I must carry you', which he borrows from Celan, 'is forever carried on the "I am", *on the sum* and *on the* cogito' [*l'emporte à jamais sur le "je suis", sur le* sum *et sur le* cogito'], for '*before being* me, I carry the other'. In that immemorial, non-originary and orificial antecedence, the *I* proceeds and precedes *itself* in fact in so far as it carries the other. This could be understood as the carrying of a burden, as the carrying of a disabled person, as a taking charge of and of course also (he thought about this) as a way of being pregnant. I carry the other in me according to the law of her division, which trembles in my bosom, and will distinguish her from me. This is how the subject *subjectivises*: by being a support of the other.

***

This also means: act in such a way so as to make reason love itself in self-love – philosophy itself, or *thought*, the weighing, the gravity, the idea of the body in its own fall. Make reason love itself up to the point where that love reveals the originary alienation, which precedes and carries it away since it is reason. The *logos*, the madness to engulf oneself in the responsibility – response and guarantee – concerning the subject [*au sujet du sujet*], concerning the one, him or her, or what will never vouch for oneself, in any heard language, but who or which will make its idiom resound sonorously 'the world has left / I must carry you' (this, then, also occurs where philosophy and poetry have the experience of each other, carry each other, both unbearable).

Patho-logy again: he suffers, he is ill from making himself heard so badly or so excessively. He prays at once in order for us to listen to him and to turn away from him: 'I must carry you' he tells the reader as much to move away as to come closer; it sounds like a call and a complaint, more like a kind of prayer. Before the utterance of *ego sum*, there is something like a prayer, like an imploration, which both welcomes the other and is weighed down by its burden – what we call love.

This imploration is everywhere in him, it ceaselessly resounds in his voice. It is the secret prayer of his discourse, to carry the other, to go out of the world by carrying the other, thus carried by him, carried away by him. The *différance* between oneself and oneself, the *différance* between the same and the same, in identity or in being, is a thought of that amorous prayer: 'I carry you and in this way, you carry me away. I pray to be delivered from me.'

Love is, for Descartes, one of the actions or properties of the *res cogitans* (alongside willing, conceiving, imagining or feeling). It consists in conjoining oneself to another up to the point of considering himself or herself as another self. An other self; an other, then, instead of the same, but also an other who is like me other from himself. An other who relates to himself by being exposed outside of self. An other who carries me away while I carry her.

This carrying away is a madness. This madness, the reason of a thought. This thought, the rigorous and consequent development of what has for so long been launched under the name of the carrying and the supporting – the *hypokeimenon*, the base, the *suppositum* [*suppôt*], the subject – the substructure and the substance of that accident which we are.

Translated by Celine Surprenant

3
Homage to Jacques Derrida

Alain Badiou

Sartre died in 1980. Since Merleau-Ponty had died before him, Sartre's death marked a closure, the closure of fifty years of French philosophy. This was the end of the period of the 1930s, of the war and the resistance, of the 1950s, of the throbbing question of relations with the Communist Party and the anti-colonial wars. After that we had the successive deaths of Lacan and Foucault, in the Eighties. Then, in the Nineties, Althusser, Lyotard and Deleuze died.

Now Jacques Derrida has died. We are before another closure: that of the philosophical generation which marked the 1960s. This is the generation whose works have best represented in writing the Sixties and mainly, perhaps, the five intense years between 1962 and 1968, between the end of the Algerian war and the revolutionary tempest of 1968–1976. Nothing more than a moment, but, truly, a moment of fulguration.

The generation of philosophers who identified that moment has almost entirely disappeared now. Only one retired tutelary figure is left, a very old man, impassible and glorious: only Claude Lévi-Strauss is still with us.

Jacques Derrida's death concludes the deaths of philosophers who 'signed' something. This is the death, the end of an historic signature, a temporal signature. My first emotion, beyond, of course, the always impressive consideration that a historic moment thus signed has disappeared, is not triumphant. My thought is: 'Now, we are the old generation.'

But whom do I mean by this 'we'? I mean precisely those of us who were the immediate disciples of those who have passed away. We, who, from 1963 to 1968, were between the ages of twenty and thirty. We, who followed with passion the lessons of these masters, we, who, following their ageing and deaths, have become now the elders. The elders not by the same rights as they, because they were the signature of the moment I am speaking about, and the present moment very probably deserves no signature. But the elders, whose youth was what it was only because they listened to and read these masters, and discussed night and day their proposals.

I even believe, I might say, if you will allow me this narcissistic touch, yes, I think I am able to say that *I am the Old Man* now. This is because I am a few years older than the rest of my generation. Here I am, in front of you, revealed as the Old Man. And the Old Man must pay homage to all those, without exception, who have, unfortunately and prematurely, passed away. Many of these men did not die really old. Old age is a relative notion: Lévi-Strauss has reached, to our great fortune, what is in our civilisation a truly great age, as did Georges Canguilhem, to cite only two of the figures of the previous generation. But those of the Sixties, the time I am talking about, did not live beyond 75, with the sole exception of Lacan. Homage must be paid to those who have passed away and who, consequently, constitute us as the elders, and constitute me as the Old Man. Not long ago, we were under their protection, despite all else. We were under their spiritual protection. They can no longer offer it to us. We are no longer separated from the real by the greatness of their voices.

I wish then, I consider it my compelling duty, to pay homage to Jacques Derrida, who has just brutally passed away, and through him, to all of them, to all the signatories of the great moment of the Sixties. In fact, whatever the great differences between them, whatever the extraordinarily violent battles they sometimes waged against each other, particularly after May 1968, we can now see clearly, and not just in the abasement that strikes so many of those who pretend to give lessons, the extent to which they were the collective signatories of an exceptional moment of thought. This does not eradicate their divergences but allows us to pronounce, for all of them and each one separately, a renewed praise through a new understanding of what they said and wrote.

Amongst the group I named above, I was, in my youth at the end of the Fifties, very close to Sartre; later, from the beginning of the Sixties, I was close to Lacan and, finally, between 1966 and 1968, to

Althusser. I was also continually at a distance from some, such as Derrida until very recently, or Foucault after 1969 and, had important and repeated quarrels as well as long periods of peace with Althusser after 1968 and, with Lyotard and Deleuze from the Seventies onwards. But my homage extends to all of them. It is addressed to the philosophical invention of an intense moment. This is altogether pertinent this evening because, as we will see later, this moment is, in some respects, still ahead of us. It is ahead of us not by means of a possible repetition, but through its reviviscence or, what I call in my language, its resurrection. A number of signs testify to this. This historic moment like all moments of its kind came to an end with the death of its signatories, those who were its heroes and emblems. But at the same time, it is also still ahead of us, in the figure of its inevitable resurrection, for it is our beacon or lantern during the confusion of our times.

I think that what constituted the moment that, like everyone else, I call 'the Sixties' – I might go so far as to call it 'the philosophical Sixties'[1] – this moment of history which culminated in a moment of action, between 1968 and 1976, is, in many respects, still 'on its feet'. I would like to pay homage to Jacques Derrida here in order to salute also this 'on your feet!'

Naturally, I would like to render a philosophical homage to Derrida, a homage inscribed or disposed within what is my mission to think. If not, it would not be the veritable homage of one philosopher to another. It would be what you have read everywhere, a journalistic or academic homage. This is indispensable because the subtlety, the quality, the innovation of Derrida's writings must be honoured and their deployment restituted. But what interests me tonight is of a different nature. I would like to try and name that point in his enterprise which I recognise absolutely, the point which, from the distance separating us, relentlessly calls on me.

A philosophical homage is a homage that indicates the interval, and gives to that interval its proper force. To do this, I need to begin with some preliminary questions, presented here in an extraordinarily simple form. This simplicity is justified. Because there was, let us not forget, just beneath the astonishing volatile fluidity of his writing, an authentic simplicity to Derrida, an obstinate and unvarying intuition. This is one of the many reasons why the violence of the attacks against him, just after his death, and in particular in the

American press, attacks against the 'abstruse thinker', 'the incomprehensible writer', were nothing more than the most banal antiintellectual insults. We shall call these insults 'Texan' and speak of them no more.

Suppose that we call 'being' – 'being' in the Heideggerian sense – just any multiplicity and that we take interest in the appearing of this being, in what permits us to say of this being that it can be seen, in some particular world. Suppose that we attempt to conceive this being, not only with respect to its Being, that is to say with respect to the pure multiplicity that constitutes its generic Being, its undetermined Being, but that we try to conceive it in the measure that it is there, with respect to its coming into this world or, its appearing on the horizon of some particular world. We shall call this appearance of a being in a world, its *existence*.

We identify being as an undifferentiated multiplicity and we take interest in its worldly horizon because this multiplicity, besides the fact of being the multiplicity it is, which is mathematically thinkable, it is also on the horizon of a world. When a being appears in a world, it exists. We find ourselves therefore within an entirely classical distinction between Being and existence. Being qua Being is what can be mathematically conceived as pure multiplicity. Existence is what can be conceived as the 'being there' of the multiplicity, on the horizon of a determined world.

The technical elaboration of a new (and integrally rational) distinction between Being and existence can take diverse forms and we will not enter into the details of this here. We will simply say that the relation between Being and 'being-there', or the relation between multiplicity and worldly inscription, is a transcendental relation. It consists in the fact that any multiplicity is assigned a degree of existence, a degree of appearance, in a world. The fact of existing, inasmuch as it is an appearance in a determined world, is inevitably associated to a degree of appearance in this world, to an intensity of appearance, which can also be called an intensity of existence.

A very complicated and important point emerges here, something to which Derrida gave some attention and in relation to which, he taught us the following: a multiplicity can appear in several different worlds. Its being-one can exist in a multiplicity. We accept the principle of the ubiquity of Being which, I would even say, is what defines humanity. Why is it that humanity can represent itself as superior to everything else it knows, if not for its capacity to appear in a great number of different worlds, to be assigned transcendentally to extraordinarily diverse intensities of existence? We exist in several worlds. And this is fortunate. If we were fixed to just one world, existence would be extraordinarily difficult, above all if the world is a sad world, as it tends to be. Fortunately, we have the capacity to exist, to be there, in a good many disparate worlds.

A multiplicity can then appear (or exist, it amounts to the same thing) in several worlds, but generally, it exists in these worlds with different degrees of intensity. It appears intensely in some world, more feebly in another, with an extreme feebleness in a third and with extraordinary intensity in a fourth. Existentially, we are perfectly acquainted with this circulation in several worlds in which we inscribe ourselves with differentiated intensities. What we call 'life', or 'our life', is often the passage from one world in which we appear with a feeble degree of intensity to a world in which this degree of existence is more intense. That is what a moment of life, a vital experience, is.

A sophisticated logic applies to all this. I am only giving you its core here. The fundamental point leading us towards Derrida's is the following. Given a multiplicity that appears in a world and given the elements of this multiplicity, these elements will naturally appear in this world too. This means that the totality of what constitutes the multiplicity appears in this world. In these conditions, it is always true that there is a component of this multiplicity, whose apparition is measured by the feeblest degree.

This is an extremely important point. I will repeat it: when a multiplicity appears in a world, the transcendental relation attributes to its elements degrees of apparition, degrees of existence. And as it happens there always exists at least one of these elements – in reality, only one exists – which appears with the feeblest degree of apparition, in other words one element exists minimally. Existing minimally in the transcendental of a world is akin to not existing at all. From the point of view of the world, if you exist as little as is possible, it is the same as not existing at all. This is why we call this element 'the inexistent'.

Given a multiplicity that appears in a world, there is always an element of this multiplicity that is an inexistent in this world. It is the inexistent proper to this multiplicity, relatively to this world.

This inexistent does not have an ontological but only an existential characterisation, it has a minimal degree of existence in a particular world. Interestingly, this can be demonstrated. We can demonstrate that, in a multiplicity that appears, there is always an element whose existence is of zero intensity. There is always a point of inexistence, as regards what exists in a world. If the multiplicity is called A, for example, the point of inexistence will be Ø, that is an empty set, index A. A proper noun and nothing else designates the inexistent of A. But it must be remembered that the inexistent of A is always the inexistent of A *in a particular world*.

Let me give you an important and well-known example. Marx argues in his analysis of bourgeois or capitalist societies that the proletariat is the inexistent specific to political multiplicities. The proletariat is 'what does not exist'. This does not mean at all that it has no Being. Marx does not think for one second that the proletariat has no Being. On the contrary he has written volume after volume to explain the proletariat. The social and economic Being of the proletariat is not uncertain. What is uncertain is its political *existence*. The proletariat is subtracted entirely from the sphere of political presentation. The multiplicity of the proletariat can be analysed, but if we consider the political world's rules of appearance, the proletariat does not appear. It is there, but with a minimal degree of appearance, a degree zero of appearance. This is obviously what the *International* states: 'We have been naught we shall be all!' What is meant by 'we have been naught'? Those who proclaim 'we have been naught' are not affirming their nothingness. They simply assert that they are nothing in the world such as it is, when it is a question of appearing politically. From the point of view of their political appearing, they are nothing. And becoming 'all' supposes changing the world, which means changing the transcendental. The transcendental must change so that the assignation to existence and the inexistent, the point of non-appearance of a multiplicity in a world, might in turn change.

Let us summarise. According to the general law of appearing or of being-there-in-a-world there is always a point of inexistence. I can now state the wager of Derrida's thought. I use the term wager strategically, in the sense of Bergson, who always said that philosophers have one single idea. For me, the wager of Derrida's work, of his infinite work, of his immense writing ramified in a number of varied works, of infinitely diverse approaches, is *to inscribe the inexistent*. Additionally, to recognise, in the work of inscribing the inexistent, that this inscription is properly speaking impossible. Derrida's stake in his writing – 'writing' designating here an act of thought – is *to inscribe the impossibility of the inscription of the inexistent as a form of its inscription*.

What does 'deconstruction' mean? Derrida was very fond of saying at the end of his life that, if there is one thing urgently in need of deconstruction, it is deconstruction, the word deconstruction itself. Once deconstruction became part of the academic repertory, it naturally had to be deconstructed. Giving a precise meaning to deconstruction amounts, in a certain sense, to dilapidating it. I think however that for Derrida, the word 'deconstruction' has not been academicised. It indicated a speculative desire, a desire for thought. A fundamental desire for thought. It was '*his*'. And the desire, like all desire, began with an encounter and a conclusion. Derrida accepted, with all the structuralists of the Sixties, with Foucault for example, that the experience of the world was always an experience of discursive imposition. Being in a world is being marked by certain discourses, marked on one's flesh, one's body, sex, etc. Derrida's thesis, Derrida's conclusion, Derrida's source of desire was that, whatever the form of discursive imposition, a point exists which escapes that imposition. We can call it the vanishing point [*point de fuite*]. This expression must be taken as literally as possible. A vanishing point is a point that, precisely, disappears from the mechanism of imposition.

Once this is accepted, the interminable aim of thought and writing is to localise this point. Localising it does not mean seizing it. 'Derrida's problem' was the following: what does it mean to seize the vanishing? This is not a question of seizing *what* is vanishing, but the vanishing as vanishing point. If you seize the vanishing, you suppress it. The vanishing point is not seizable as such. It can only be localised.

Derrida proposes something resembling a gesture of (de)monstration. He carries out a gesture of writing with his finger dipped into white ink. Such writing will delicately show the vanishing point, while at the same time letting it vanish. The vanishing point cannot be shown as such, it cannot be shown as if dead. This is what Derrida fears above all else: showing the vanishing point as dead.

One should show the vanishing point without the vanishing. This is why Derrida develops a type of writing, which will attempt to become a monstration. I call this localisation, because to show is to localise. One has to say: 'Shh!... it might be there, careful!... it might be there... don't make it stop... let it vanish.'

Derrida is the opposite of the hunter. The hunter hopes that the animal will stop so he can shoot it. He hopes that he can put an end to the vanishing of the animal. Derrida, hopes that the vanishing will not cease to vanish, that the 'thing' (the vanishing point) will be shown in its evidence without any interruption of its vanishing, in its incessant disappearing. The textual stake of Derrida's desire is that all appearance is sustained by a (dis)appearance, only the vanishing of which can be localised in the forest of sense.

But localising the vanishing point – to say nothing of seizing it, which would be its death – is, in fact, impossible. This is because the vanishing point is what, within a place (*lieu*), is outside that place (*hors-lieu*). It is the outside within. Because the vanishing point exists only in its act beyond the place, it is not possible to localise it exactly. To show the vanishing one has to penetrate deep into the forest that localises it. During the walk, you learn that you cannot show the vanishing; at most you can show, from a fair distance, the localisation of the vanishing, a thicket or clearing. This already is very risky.

Finally, what is perhaps possible is to restrain the space of the vanishing, to go through the forest a little more loyally, or a little less obscurely. If you do not want to intrude into the vanishing, the localisation consists in simply seeing to it that the discursive imposition, the language constraints are not such that the vanishing space covers the whole. In that case, you would localise nothing inexistent and you would have instead the space of the general. Even so, you must restrain your walking space in order to be close to the spot where the vanishing takes place. You should be in a place as close as possible to what is excepted from the place, what is found outside. Deconstruction, in reality, consists in restraining the discursive operations in such a way that the space of the vanishing is localisable as on a map, by saying: 'The treasure is there or, the source is there. What is going away is there but tread softly, very softly... If not, the treasure will be purloined, the source will no longer flow. I have a map, but it is vague, vague enough to avoid stepping on the treasure...One step on the treasure and it is no longer worth anything. Even chance is risky...tread softly.'

Take for example the great metaphysical oppositions. They must be turned from opposites to diagonals in order to restrict the discursive space and not allow the massive, linear massiveness, subsist. The outside of the place of important binary oppositions cannot be localised. Instead, they must be deconstructed. Our path must pass by them. This is deconstruction. Deconstruction is, fundamentally, the set of operations, which can restrict somehow the space of the vanishing, the space where the vanishing point is found. This operation resembles again a reversed hunt, in which what must be seized is the healthy animal disappearing, the animal's leap beyond the hunter's grasp. This is why you must get as close to it as possible. Perhaps, even closer than is necessary in order to shoot. This is why you must have a patient localisation. Localisation supposes an elementary map of the major distinctions, between city and country, mountain and valley, Being and being, and this blocking out must be reduced step by step.

This leads to a whole series of debates such as the argument with Heidegger, for example, on the effective relevance of the difference between Being and being. When Derrida proposes the concept of '*différance*', he wants us to hear in it a unique term that would activate the distinction between Being and being at its vanishing point. Derrida renders evanescent the element of a metaphysical opposition that subsists in the Being/being difference, so that we might grasp difference as such, *in its act. Différance*, in its action, lies at the vanishing point of all opposition between Being and being, it is what can in no way be reduced to the figure of this opposition. Following this and in the same way, the opposition between democracy and totalitarianism must be examined or, alternatively, that between Jew and Arab in the Palestinian conflict. The method is always the same. Examining the opposition Jew/Arab in the Palestinian conflict, Derrida's position was to deconstruct the duality. On each occasion, the method is to examine an opposition that prematurely certifies its place as division, partition or classification and discover what marks that place instead as the territory of a vanishing point.

Derrida declassifies classified affairs.

Derrida was involved in campaigns which call for, what I call, a courageous man of peace. He was courageous because, in a certain sense, a great deal of courage is always necessary in order to avoid accepting and entering a division as constituted. A man of peace, because the detection of what is beyond a constituted opposition is, generally, the way of peace and of thought.

This diagonal obstinacy, this refusal of abrupt partitions of meta-physical origin, does not suit tempestuous times, when everything is submitted to a law of decision, here and now. This is what kept Derrida outside of the truth of the 'red years' between 1968 and 1976. The (Maoist) truth of those years insisted that 'one can be divided into two'. This statement expresses poetically the metaphys-ics of radical conflict rather than the patient deconstruction of oppo-sitions. Derrida could not follow in that; he had to go away. We might say he exiled himself to America. This is because Derrida was consistent in his literal patience. Although he did not ignore the vio-lence of true patience, he possessed a great speculative gentleness. This was the Derridean touch.

His great book on and with Jean-Luc Nancy, published in 2000, is called *On Touching: Jean-Luc Nancy*.[2] It was a wonderful book, Derri-da's 'treatise on the soul', his treatise on sensations, his most delight-fully Aristotelian book. Derrida wants to give a new description of the relationship between the sensuous and thought. Here too, in the opposition between the sensuous and thought, we must find the vanishing point. The touch is something like that. Something so delicately sensitive that it becomes indiscernible to thought.

This is why Derrida increasingly used the form of the dialogue. Dialogues with Hélène Cixous,[3] Elisabeth Roudinesco,[4] Jürgen Haber-mas and others.[5] Many of these debates are with what one could call the feminine position. In a debate with a heteronomous position, one may touch, perhaps, what escapes the Law, what makes a supple bound outside the *nomos*. You may be caressed by it *on the way.*

It is this spirit of the passing caress that interested me in the great debate Derrida carried out with psychoanalysis. The entry point of this debate was the vanishing point in the opposition between mas-culine and feminine. What is outside of this opposition? Psycho-analysis offered ample material to discuss this question. In truth, Derrida was on a quest for the feminine touch of thought. He had an interlocution with the possibility of a feminine singularity in the trajectory of whoever attempts to think.

Derrida liked confronting, in the form of his texts, a certain delicateness, a literary subtlety, with something philosophically somewhat rough. These two were not exclusive for him, one or the other. This is why you come across a very strange pair in *Glas*, the couple Genet and Hegel.[6] Why this couple? It pairs an extremely sophisticated prose with an unprecedented conceptual rudeness. Derrida manages to show that this opposition – rough and impenetrable conceptuality, on the one hand, and totally perverse literary sinuosity, on the other – composes the possibility of localising the vanishing point in writing.

I return now to my preliminary point. I should say, somewhat in the manner of Lacan, that the inexistent, the void indexed on A, is precisely Derrida's object of desire, his considerable and null speculative 'object a'. His desire to think is constituted there, in the sense that it is a desire within thought. Yes, what Derrida desired was the inexistent.

When one desires something, what does he do with it? This desire, this desire for the inexistent, this inexistent, necessarily, like all desire must be put down somewhere, in the end. Placed on the table, for example, even though one knows that it is already on its feet. It is already somewhere else, already gone. Such was Derrida's desire: localise, touch, embrace, for even less than an instant, the inexistent of a place, the vanishing of the vanishing point.

Despite appearances, there is no relation between this desire and Lacan's woman, who does not exist. Not existing is precisely the logical mode of existence for Lacan's woman. But we are not talking about existence here. It is inexistence we are discussing, the degree zero of existence, because it is a zero degree of appearance, what does not appear in a world.

But be careful! You cannot say of the inexistent that it is nothingness. This is the whole difficulty, where the metaphysical error lies, the only metaphysical error that cannot be remedied. The metaphysical error *par excellence* is to identify the inexistent with nothingness. This is because the inexistent precisely *is*. It is absolutely. That is why the proletarians, who *inexist*, can fight for their Being and say: 'We have been naught we shall be all!' This is the definition of the Revolution: an inexistent argues for its multiple-Being in order to declare that it shall be absolutely. To be sure, for that to happen we must change the world, the transcendental of the world.

The inexistent is *nothing*. But being nothing is not at all not being anything. Being nothing is to *inexist* in a way proper to a given world or place. Thus the alternate shifts that characterised Derrida's prose become clear. There is a sliding between the two statements, 'if you say the inexistent *is*, you naturally miss that it does not exist', and 'if you are content to say it does not exist, you miss that it *is*'. As a result, no constituted opposition manages to qualify the exact status of the inexistent in the terms of a binary opposition. Because you are always sliding from Being to inexistence and, then, from inexistence to Being. Derrida's logic no longer authorises the fundamental distinction between affirmation and negation.

What underlies the question and brings deconstruction to its term is when the logical space in which one operates is no longer the space of the opposition between affirmation and negation. I would say that the touch is like that. The touch is a logical operator. When you touch something, you are and you are not that thing. This is the whole drama of the amorous caress. The ideal of deconstruction is to relate to a text or to a political situation in the way the amorous caress is logically related to a body. An ideal of the touch. With the touch, what touches is separated from what is touched only by an inexistence, an unassignable vanishing point. What differentiates the two 'actors' of the touch, the active and the passive, is only the act of touching, which, precisely, is also what conjoins them. Thus we have this sliding, what I call the essential sliding, the sliding between being and existing. This is the major sliding that has the inexistent as its sign and hook.

Derrida has installed this sliding within language. This is my last remark. Derrida attempted to say that a genuine word is a sliding. A word is not a reference, nor a signifier, it is a sliding, a sliding between being and existence. A word resonates just when it slides according to the inexistent. 'Slide mortals, do not insist!', Derrida would say to his own words. That is why he was so criticised. He irritated me too sometimes by his extraordinary verbal acrobatics, the infinite sliding of his prose. But we can also render justice to that, because the demonstration of the sliding bears the desire of the inexistent. To reveal the vanishing point you must make the language fly away. You must have a vanishing language. You can only organise in language a (de)monstration of the inexistent, if you use a language that can bear to *inexist*. An evanescent language. And in that case, as Genet said, 'my victory is verbal'.

My ultimate homage will also be verbal.

In homage to Derrida, I will say and write from now on *inexistance* with an 'a'. Inexist*a*nce. As he said différ*a*nce. And, after all, very close to what he wanted to say when he invented, a very long time ago, the word différ*a*nce. The word différ*a*nce is basically the operation through which Jacques Derrida attempted to put inexistence down. To put it down as you put something down in writing. He tried to put down the inexistent in the différ*a*nce as an act of writing, as a sliding. In imitation of Derrida, I will also attempt to put down inexistence, by imposing the sliding from 'e' to 'a', which signifies, in its worldly manner of *inexisting* that its being is nonetheless irreducible. We are naught, let us be. This is the imperative of inexist*a*nce. There is no way out of that.

Notes

1. TN: In English in the text.
2. J. Derrida, *Le toucher – Jean-Luc Nancy* (Paris: Galilée, 2000). [Translated by C. Irizarry: J. Derrida, *On Touching: Jean-Luc Nancy* (Stanford: Stanford University Press, 2005)].
3. H. Cixous, J. Derrida, *Voiles*, trans. G. Bennington (Stanford: Stanford University Press, 2001).
4. J. Derrida, E. Roudinesco, *For What Tomorrow…A Dialogue*, trans. J. Fort (Stanford: Stanford University Press, 2004).
5. G. Borradori, *Philosophy in a Time of Terror: Dialogues with Jürgen Habermas and Jacques Derrida* (Chicago: Chicago University Press, 2003).
6. J. Derrida, *Glas*, trans. J. P. Leavey and R. Rand (Lincoln: University of Nebraska Press, 1990).

4
Notes Towards a Tribute to Jacques Derrida

Gayatri Chakravorty Spivak

The public part of mourning is a not unimportant step in the releas-
ing of the ghost in us. We cannot know the gift, least of all a gift
coming from a named ghost. We know the gift, if there is any, as
responsibility, accountability. I will follow that line in this instal-
ment of my mourning work.

Derrida was always mindful of sexual difference. The project of
sexual difference can now be summarised as: catch the mother. I, the
son, am the mother's trace, and the father's sign. Mindful of sexual
difference, Derrida was also mindful of what kind of seeker or inves-
tigator he could be. I now understand why the daughter's quest could
not be staged by him. Although the books on democracy (*Politics of
Friendship, Rogues*) are full of worries about women, the book on
Marx (*Specters of Marx*) is without a trace of what one would recognise as feminism, as indeed is the book on the lovely photographs of
the lesbian lovers.[1] (That last book is all about how photographs are
'meaning-full' and what such meanings can be.)

If we were speaking about feminism and Derrida, I would stand
by my two early essays on the subject: 'Displacement and the
Discourse of Woman' (1983), and 'Feminism and Deconstruction,
Again' (1989).[2] 'At whatever remove of "différance"... *sexual difference is thought*, sexual *differential* between "man" and "woman"
remains irreducible;' and, 'we have to... neutralize the name of
"woman" *for deconstruction* and be deconstructive feminists in that
sense'.[3]

Derrida's book on the postcard can be read as being about making
a child.[4] *Glas*, the book on the queer Genet was an attempt to catch

'her,' the mother in the metronymic, 'elle' in French, a big L-shaped blank in the text toward the end of the book. Genet did not know his father, he was a mother's child.[5] *Glas* was also a mourning book for the author's father. One gesture of the book is to try out the newly inherited patronymic as a meaningful sign rather than a mark. (A mark indicates a person, bypassing the sign-system. The word 'Beatrice,' for example, is not withdrawn from the system of meanings, but, in so far as it refers to a named individual, it is a mark.) It was as if Jacques Derrida, who was no longer the sign of the name or mark of the father but, with the death of the father, held the patronymic, was curious to see how much control he had over the name, not as mark but as sign.

One of these many phrases breaking down the proper name Derrida sticks in my mind: Dionysos Erigone Eriopétale Réséda![6] In those years, the early and mid-Seventies, many such semiotic games were played with the patronymic. One of the titles of Derrida's book on the Italian artist Adami, for example, was *Derrière le rideau* – behind the curtain: an expansion of the patronymic that made it mean mystery.[7]

Glas was also a strong critique of reproductive heteronormativity (RHN) as represented by the Holy Family and Hegel's discourse of the state. Indeed, the critique of RHN fitted in within the general critique of phallocentrism. But the matter of the mother's child carried a salutary moment within the critique. Let us remind ourselves of the child in *The Post Card* and of Jean Genet in *Glas*. I will risk a generalisation: Derrida slips the trace into RHN.

RHN offers the grounding propositions or *Grundsätze* for the tremendously heterogeneous performative conventions of all cultures, through time. The word 'performative' is used more broadly here than in J. L. Austin's definition.[8] Let us say it means 'a system of meaning that makes words do things.' When Derrida suggests, as he did throughout his work, that the event is what escapes the performative, it is in this broader sense that he is making this claim. (What escapes the performative stereotypes of reproductive heteronormativity is the singularity of the event. The implications for feminisms are immense here. But, as I have indicated in my early essays, Derrida's task was not to follow up these implications. Our question will therefore be confined to what it might mean to invade RHN with trace-thinking.)

What, then, is a trace? It is or is not, or, more importantly, is in the possibility of always not being, the material suggestion that something else was there before, something other than it, of course. Unlike a sign, which carries a systemic assurance of meaning, a trace carries no guarantees. Animal spoor on the forest floor (in German trace is *Spur*) may mean the animal was there, that it's a decoy, that I am mistaken or hallucinating, and so on. When I am around, you know I had a mother, but that is all. There is no guarantee who that mother was, except that she was a Mme. Derrida. I am my mother's trace. The Father's name is written within the patronymic sign system.

Let us read a description of taking care of something like a trace in some important paragraphs of Kant. Kant put a line through fourteen paragraphs in his own copy of the first edition of *The Critique of Pure Reason*.[9] In the second edition he added two opening paragraphs, but kept the fourteen deleted paragraphs as they were. In my fancy, they are forever 'under erasure,' making visible the mechanical (in the eighteenth century?) undergirdings of a method to which Kant's language usually gives a more philosophising (though not psychologising) cast.[10] And it is here that Kant seems to admit to the idea that his task as a philosopher is to bring under control something as indecisive as a trace:

> since there is still something that follows, I must necessarily relate it to something else in general that precedes, and on which it follows in accordance with a rule, i.e. necessarily, so that the occurrence, as the conditioned, yields a secure indication of some condition, but it is the latter [the condition] that determines the occurrence.[11]

(We should note that occurrence here is *Begebenheit*, with the connotation of a given, rather than *was geschieht* in the passage quoted in note 10, with the connotation of something taking place, which is also translated 'occurrence.')

Kant is talking about the apprehension of sequence as causality. The philosopher must have the apprehension of an objective sequence, because otherwise the subjective apprehension of sequence would be 'entirely undermined'.[12] And what is the object that will yield objectivity? By the dry logic of these fourteen paragraphs, Kant gives an altogether impersonal answer: 'That in the appearance which contains the condition of th[e] necessary rule of apprehension [that distinguishes it from every other apprehension] is the object.'[13] We are looking at the management of the undermining risk of the trace. Later Kant will tell us that the object that will give us real objectivity 'cannot be given through any experience...' and we must 'regard all the concatenation [*Verknüpfung*] of things in the world of sense *as if* they had their ground in [an entity created by reason functioning rationally].'[14]

If we want to follow this line of thought, this trace, so to speak, we can even suggest that Derrida puts the trace in the place of transcendental deduction. Here is Kant:

> To seek an empirical deduction of [space, time, and the concepts of understanding] would be entirely futile work, for what is distinctive in their nature is precisely that they are related to their objects without having borrowed anything from experience for their thinking [*Vorstellung*]. Thus if a deduction of them is necessary, it must always be transcendental....A tracing [*Nachspüren*] of the first strivings [*Bestrebungen*] of our power of cognition to ascend from individual perceptions to general concepts is without doubt of great utility....Yet a *deduction* of the pure *a priori* concepts can never be achieved in this way; it does not lie down this path at all, for in regard to their future use, which should be entirely independent of experience, an entirely different birth certificate than that of an engendering [*Abstammung*] from experiences must be produced.[15]

We cannot not notice that the question of securing a better birth certificate (transcendental deduction) than a mere tracing of experiential birth is all too clear. A fatherly origin, not a motherly engendering.

When Derrida wrote in 1968 that 'I have attempted to indicate a way out of the closure of this framework via the "trace,"' he was ostensibly speaking of Saussure's espousing of language as causeless effect. 'In and of itself, outside its text [*hors texte*], it is not sufficient to operate the necessary transgression,' the paragraph closes.[16] I suggest that 'transcendental deduction' can be put in the place of 'transgression' and it would make sense. For Kant closes off ('the closure of a framework') the trace by transcendental deduction.

I therefore think that it is the connection of the 'as if' with the suppression of the trace-structure in the interest of the more secure birth certificate of the transcendental deduction, establishing the performative conventions of philosophy, as it were, that makes Derrida write, nearly forty years later, in a section subtitled 'the Neutralisation of the Event,' that the idea of a 'world,' as in 'worlding' or 'globalisation,' is itself one of those architechtonic trace-stopping event-neutralising 'as if'-s in Kant's thought.[17]

To follow this line would take us away from any recognisable task of feminisms in brief compass. As we have noticed, in the discourse on democracy, women are never forgotten, but invoked only as a trace of the many 'outsides' of democracy. Let us pause for a moment on that threshold before we return to the terrain of feminisms.

In the passage where Derrida reminds us that the world is an 'as if' in Kant, he is cautioning those who would find the model of a correct democracy today in Kant, to remember that nothing in Kant can be entertained without considering the entire architectonic. And indeed, if the general reader follows the structural hints from the talk of the 'as if'-s, she or he is struck by the relentless honesty that makes Kant think the transcendental deduction: because we are programmed to insist that experience is possible. We are scared with the possibility that there is radical heterogeneity between the deduction and the evidence produced by experience. As Derrida reminds us in the middle of his book, 'to speak democratically of democracy, on the subject of democracy, to speak of democracy in an intelligible, univocal, and *directed* way, would be to make oneself understood by *anyone who can* understand the word or the sentences one makes with the word.'[18] That discourse cannot be offered by Immanuel Kant, who believed the publishing scholar to be the subject of the Enlightenment.

As Derrida chases a democracy to come, he obliquely urges the general reader to do a bit of reading for which there is no time now: 'If the time had been given to me for it, I would have tried to follow here the thread that runs from *Vom Wesen des Grundes* (1929), in particular around the concept of "world" and its history, up to *Der Satz vom Grund* (1957).'[19]

One cannot of course follow Derrida's injunction, interminably, here. Let us just open Heidegger's *On the Essence of Ground* (hereafter cited as EG).[20] If Kant had instituted transcendental deduction to close off the uncertainty of something like a trace while marking its authority as the source of the unaccountable synthetic *a priori*, Heidegger redefines the transcendental as the impersonal structure of the *Dasein*, assuring its prior projection into the world. In thus changing the allure of Kant, Heidegger notes the importance of one of the passages I quote above, the passage under Kant's manual erasure, as it were: 'It is certainly the case that one commonly finds a lack of any explicit treatment of the "principle of reason" in his "critical" writings, unless one allows the proof of the second analogy to count as substitute for this almost incomprehensible shortcoming' (EG 106–7). However, where Kant cautiously distinguishes between universality and totality and makes only the latter available, and even then through a synthesis of intuition; and allows only the minor premise of a syllogism to be available to the understanding and insists the major premise to be a synthetic judgement and then allows a restricted definition of the pure concept of reason, Heidegger, quoting restrictively, offers a less complex and more continuous conclusion: 'as thinkings [*Vorstellungen*] of the unconditioned totality of a realm of beings, ideas are necessary thinkings [*Vorstellungen*]' (*Critique of Pure Reason* 399–400, EG 117). Where Kant systematically cautions against speculation, Heidegger, collapsing universality and totality, uses the word 'speculative' as if it is merely the positive colloquial usage and calls the '"transcendental ideal"... [the] highest point of Kant's speculative metaphysics'(EG 118–19). This is just to give a sense of how Heidegger undoes Kant's critical circumscriptions in claiming a pre-emptive world-projection for *Dasein* before it has become *existentiell*. I will follow through on Derrida's reading instructions in detail elsewhere. The point here is to note that, for Derrida, attention to the trace in thinking democracy for a world brings us back to the early thought of thought, here, now, as a textual blank. The reading of this thought is to come and that is the responsibility of thinking. Especially the thinking of democracy.

In an interesting response to Robert Gooding's essay 'Race, Multiculturalism, and Democracy,' Judith Butler establishes solidarity with him by saying that as philosophy graduate students at

Yale in the Eighties, they had embraced the Hegelian logic of constitutivity.[21] In the Preface to the 1999 edition of *Subjects of Desire*, Butler writes: 'In a sense, all of my work remains within the orbit of a certain set of Hegelian questions: What is the relation between desire and recognition, and how is it that the constitution of the subject entails a radical and constitutive relation to alterity?'[22]

This sense of constitutivity which many of us, including Laclau and Mouffe, share is closer to the everyday sense of the self–other dialectic. When we place 'regulative' over against this, it means something like that which 'regulates', as with a definitive norm, or an invocation of essence. I have myself used 'regulative' in this more everyday sense in 'regulative psychobiography'.[23] In Kant, the use of 'constitutive' and 'regulative' is more idiosyncratic.

Kant thinks that even pure understanding has no access to the system of reason which governs its function except by analogising with the schemata of the senses, with one important distinction: whereas the schemata of the senses lead to empirical knowledge, the analogical relationship that the understanding must establish with reason leads to no empirical knowledge. It is within these constraints that the understanding can set up two kinds of analogies: constitutive and regulative.

The constitutive analogy of the understanding is mathematical, where if two members are given, the third can be 'constructed'. The regulative analogy can only give relations and approximations. All reasoning, including philosophy, operated under this 'as if'. The paragraphs under erasure that we read belong to the second analogy of the understanding – which produces the intuition that time is a caused sequence. Those unrevised paragraphs reveal the geometrical impersonality of Kant's reasoning. The regulative leans toward the constitutive.

When a Luce Irigaray speaks of the empty space of the sexuate, binding it nonetheless to rights; or, a Derrida of the mode of 'to come', bending it nonetheless to democracy, they are chasing an event which is the name of what escapes the use of performative conventions that permit the production of even regulative analogies.[24] The 'use of gender' – the use of performative conventions of the stereotypes of reproductive heteronormativity, even to question them, would remain within the constraints of something like Kant's regulative analogies, analogising from body as writing to mind as reader.

If I am on the right track, the project of feminism is not unrelated to, but elsewhere from Derrida's child-trace of mother. The project of feminism remains within the approximations of the regulative. Derrida's questions chase the trace: What am I as trace? What shall I mourn when my mother dies? I have touched on the obsession with how am I a signified, now that I hold the name of the father, in *Glas*. It is no surprise that the tracking of the trace of the mother is laid to rest in 'Circumfession,' the wrenching mourning text written at Derrida's mother's death.[25]

Unlike *Glas*, 'Circumfession' is not a book. It is only the contradiction at the foot of a book, as a running unconnected footnote to the project of fixing the nature of the patronymic once and for all, in a book called *Jacques Derrida*, that authoritative part written by another person, Geoffrey Bennington. 'Circumfession' is not part of the title; it is excessive to the architectonic of the book in Derrida's name. 'But what is it to be correct about deconstruction? I am reminded of the game you played in "Circumfession", unravelling Geoff's impeccable account of deconstruction like a Ulysses playing at Penelope,' I said to Derrida at his seventieth birthday party.[26] Perhaps, then, he was following a female lead? At any rate, the project was also to undo what Bennington would summarise as 'Derrida's thought', to provide a counter-example, day by day, only as long as the computer would allow, not, in other words, by the energy of his own thinking.[27]

I have written about 'Circumfession' in greater detail elsewhere.[28] Here let me say that the sons who animate that text (Derrida and the other Franco-Maghrebin Augustine, who wrote about the loss of his mother, who just happened to be called Santa Monica, the name also of a section of Los Angeles where Derrida often was in his mourning-time, such is the associative illogic of trace-writing), caught within circumcision, actual or 'of the heart', could not mourn the mother.[29]

In closing, I want to move to the text which introduced me to Derrida, and to the long footnote to Melanie Klein to be found there. In the passage in *Of Grammatology* that opens the footnote, Derrida writes of the same things that Kant was writing about in those paragraphs under erasure: 'the originary constitution of objectivity and the value of the object – the constitution of *good* and *bad* objects as categories that do not let themselves be derived from a formal *theoretical* ontology and from a science of the objectivity of the object in general'. He is commenting on psychoanalysis, of course. Notice how, in continuing, the language of transcendentality and the archi-trace under erasure connects with the argument I am constructing: 'even if psychoanalysis does not get to the transcendentality – under erasure – of the archi-trace, even if it remained a worldly science, its generality would have an archontic sense with regard to all regional sciences'.[30]

Considering the question of the originary constitution of objectivity, Kant was obliged to describe and control something like the trace-structure with the analogical and architectonic 'as if' of the transcendental deduction, a better and certified birth. It is in Melanie Klein that Derrida finds, that early on, the assurance of constructing the object within the trace of a life, the subject's history, rather than the 'as if' of the regulative use of reason bolstered up by transcendental deduction.

In 1967, I had not yet read Kant with care (and so could not make the connection), but Derrida had. I went on to be fascinated by Klein 'on my own'. Reading Klein with care, some years ago I summarised my sense of her as follows. The passage will be carried by the concept-metaphor of 'translation', for that was the subject on which I had been asked to speak. Yet I cannot forget that the work on Melanie Klein was going to go toward an essay on the graphic of the gift, in an anthology that never materialised. Two self-quotations here, then, neither of which concatenates with the thought of the gift. After the passage on Klein and/as translation, a passage on mother and nation as giving the gift of life, the metapsychological as allegory of reading.

1. In every possible sense, translation is necessary but impossible. Melanie Klein, the Viennese psychoanalyst whom the Bloomsbury Group killed with kindness, suggested that the work of translation is an incessant shuttle that is a 'life'.[31] The human infant grabs on to some one thing and then things. This grabbing [*begreifen*] of an outside indistinguishable from an inside constitutes an inside, going back and forth and coding everything into a sign-system by the thing(s) grasped. One can call this crude coding a 'translation'. In this never-ending weaving, violence

translates into conscience and vice versa. From birth to death this 'natural' machine, programming the mind perhaps as genetic instructions programme the body (where does body stop and mind begin?) is partly meta-psychological and therefore outside the grasp of the mind. Thus 'nature' passes and re-passes into 'culture', in a work or shuttling site of violence: the violent production of the precarious subject of reparation and responsibility. To plot this weave, the reader – in my estimation, Klein was more a reader than an analyst in the strict Freudian sense – translating the incessant translating shuttle into that which is read, must have the most intimate knowledge of the rules of representation and permissible narratives which make up the substance of a culture, and must also become responsible and accountable to the writing/translating presupposed original.

When so-called ethno-philosophies describe the embedded ethico-cultural subject being formed prior to the terrain of rational decision-making, they are dismissed as fatalistic. But the insight, that the constitution of the subject in responsibility is a certain kind of translation, of a genealogical scripting, which is not under the control of the deliberative consciousness, is not something that just comes from Melanie Klein. What is interesting about Melanie Klein is that she does indeed want to touch responsibility-based ethical systems rather than just rights-based ethical systems and therefore she looks at the violent translation that constitutes the subject in responsibility. It is in this sense that the human infant, on the cusp of the natural and the cultural, is in translation, except the word translation loses its dictionary sense right there. Here, the body itself is a script – or perhaps one should say a ceaseless inscribing instrument.[32]

2.   A general temporising of narrative enables individual and collective life. When we are born, we are (born into) the possibility of timing: temporalisation. This possibility we can grasp only by temporising – thinking and feeling a before, which through a now, will fall due in an after. Our (mother) languaging seems almost coeval with this, for we are also born into it. Since it has a before before us, we take from its already-there-ness. And since we can give meaning in it, we can think ourselves into the falling-due of the future. It is this thought, of giving and taking, that is

the idiomatic story of time into which the imposition of 'identities' must be accommodated.

Since it is usually our mothers who seem to bring us into temporalisation, our temporising often marks that particular intuition of origin by coding and recoding the mother, by computing possible futures through investing or manipulating womanspace. The daughtership of the nation is bound up with that very recoding. Nation and Mother are transcendental names for the gift of time. It is precisely making up, the theatricality of the everyday, an alteration of the national self in iteration, upon which the migrant woman committed to a national origin must turn her back (or, which comes to the same thing, must extend the warmest embrace, as in 'ethnic dressing').[33] The generations – and the mother recoded by different intuitions of origin, different projects of temporising – will ring the changes on this disavowal, a chain of displacements yet once again. What disappears and yet lingers, as common sense, is that womanly cosmopolitanism in exogamy that survives as mere common sense. It is this that gives way, again and again, to the simulacrum of a national voice.

The idea of Mother and Nation as ingredients of an ethical semiotic can be broken down into a time before time if one reads Melanie Klein carefully.[34] By contrast, Freud's invocation of Mother and Nation/God remains grounded in the fetishistic character of a grounding error.[35]

These self-quotations give an indication of some of the ways in which the agency in feminism emerged for me, rearranging reproductive heteronormativity into a field of traces in its deepest generality, via Klein, to work with children for a democracy to come, literalising Derrida. It is the part of Derrida that makes me know the limits of such regulative work. It is in the unnameable name of the event that I have proposed the methodological convenience of the separation of agency and subjecthood: regulation and the trace.

Have I acknowledged my debt right?

At the end of 'To do Justice to Freud', his mourning-essay on Foucault, Derrida writes: 'I am trying, since this is, unfortunately, the only recourse left us in the solitude of questioning, to imagine the principle of the reply;' and goes on to say, as I too will: 'I would venture to wager that, in a sentence that I will not construct for him, he would have associated and yet also dissociated', he who would not speak for what I am.

Notes

1. Jacques Derrida, *Politics of Friendship*, trans. George Collins (New York: Verso, 1994); *Rogues: Two Essays on Reason*, trans. Pascale-Anne Brault and Michael Naas (Stanford: Stanford University Press, 2005; *Specters of Marx: the State of the Debt, the Work of Mourning, and the New International,* trans. Peggy Kamuf (New York: Routledge, 1994); *Right of Inspection,* trans. David Wills (New York: Monacelli, 1998).
2. Gayatri Chakravorty Spivak, 'Displacement and the Discourse of Woman', in Mark Krupnick (ed.) *Displacement: Derrida and After* (Bloomington: Indiana University Press, 1983); 'Feminism and Deconstruction Again', in T. Brennan (ed.) *Between Feminism and Psychoanalysis* (New York: Routledge, 1989).
3. Spivak, 'Displacement', p. 184, 'Feminism', p. 218.
4. Jacques Derrida, *The Post Card: from Socrates to Freud and Beyond*, trans. Alan Bass (Chicago: University of Chicago Press, 1987).
5. Jacques Derrida, *Glas*, trans. J. P. Leavey, Jr. and R. Rand (Lincoln: University of Nebraska Press, 1986). I have discussed these thematics in detail in '*Glas*-piece: A *Compte-rendu*', in *Diacritics*, 7.3 (Fall 1977).
6. I gave a more psychoanalytic reading of this in Spivak, '*Glas*-piece', p. 24: 'I can read *déjà* as a fictive cryptonym – for the always already assumed ground of the self that can never yet be grasped; read *derrière les rideaux* as a cryptic rebus for the name of the father, the *same* as one's own, but not quite; or read "Dionysos Erigone Eriopétale Réséda" as his own name crypted in the language of Genet's flowers.' *Otobiographies*, translated as *The Ear of the Other: Otobiography, Transference, Translation*, trans. Peggy Kamuf (New York: Schocken, 1985), where the mother as blood and the father as law was to be spelled out via Nietzsche, was not yet written. And Derrida's mother was, of course, living.
7. Jacques Derrida, 'Valerio Adami: Le Voyage du Dessin', *Derrière le Mirroir*, 214 (Paris: Maeght, 1975).
8. J. L. Austin, *How to Do Things With Words* (Cambridge, MA: Harvard University Press, 1962).
9. I. Kant, *Critique of Pure Reason*, trans. Paul Guyer and Alan W. Wood (Cambridge: Cambridge University Press, 1998) 305–11.
10. The translators have a difficult time with this particular aspect of Kant, of course. But in the course of these paragraphs, even the most astute translators make curious decisions. For '*so stellet sich etwas vor*' (something thus sets itself out), we read 'I represent something;' '*was da geschieht*' becomes 'an occurrence' rather than 'what takes place there' (Guyer and Wood, p. 310). '*Anschauung*' is translated 'experience' rather

than 'intuition' in the crucial sentence 'by means of the understanding the very same order and constant connection in the series of possible perceptions is produced and made necessary as would be encountered *a priori* in the form of inner intuition (time)' (Guyer and Wood, p. 311).

11. Kant, *Pure Reason*, p. 307.
12. *Idem.*
13. Ibid. p. 306.
14. Ibid. p. 611; Kant's emphasis.
15. Ibid. pp. 220–1.
16. Jacques Derrida, 'Différance', in Alan Bass, trans. *Margins of Philosophy* (Chicago: University of Chicago Press, 1982) 12.
17. Derrida, *Rogues*, p. 121.
18. Ibid. p. 71; translation modified.
19. Ibid. p. 171; translation modified.
20. M. Heidegger, 'On the Essence of Ground', trans. William McNeill, in William McNeill (ed.) *Pathmarks* (Cambridge; Cambridge University Press, 1998). Hereafter cited in text as EG, with page numbers following.
21. J. Butler, 'Reply to Robert Gooding-Williams', 5/1 *Constellations*, 1998, 42–7.
22. J. Butler, *Subjects of Desire: Hegelian Reflections in Twentieth-Century France*, 2nd edn. (New York: Columbia University Press, 1999) xiv.
23. Gayatri Chakravorty Spivak, *A Critique of Postcolonial Reason: toward the History of the Vanishing Present* (Cambridge, MA: Harvard University Press, 1999) 298 and passim.
24. L. Irigaray, 'The Necessity for Sexuate Rights, and How to Define Sexuate Rights?' in Margaret Whitford (ed.) *The Irigaray Reader* (Oxford: Blackwell, 1991) 198–203, 204–12.
25. Jacques Derrida, 'Circumfession', in Jacques Derrida and Geoffrey Bennington, *Jacques Derrida*, trans. Geoffrey Bennington (Chicago: University of Chicago Press, 1993).
26. Gayatri Chakravorty Spivak, 'Touched by Deconstruction', 20 *Greyroom*, Summer 2005, 95–104.
27. I never did work out what the limit of the computer meant.
28. Gayatri Chakravorty Spivak, 'Three Women's Texts and Circumfession', in A. Hornung and E. Ruhe (eds) *Postcolonialism and Autobiography* (Amsterdam: Rodopi, 1998) 7–22. *Critical Inquiry* rejected the piece that was only on 'Circumfession' as insufficiently elaborated. One of these days...
29. Epistle to the Romans 2.25–29. Christians, unlike Jews, are exhorted by Paul to be circumcised in the heart rather than in the flesh.
30. Jacques Derrida, *Of Grammatology*, trans. Gayatri Chakravorty Spivak (Baltimore: Johns Hopkins University Press, 1976) 88; translation modified.
31. What follows is my own interpretative digest of Melanie Klein, *Works* (New York: Free Press, 1984), Vols. 1–4. Giving specific footnotes is

therefore impossible. The details may also not resemble orthodox Kleinian psychoanalysis.
32. Gayatri Chakravorty Spivak, 'Translation as Culture', in I. Carrera Suárez et al. (eds) *Translating Cultures* (Oviedo: Dangaroo Press, 1999) 17–30; reprinted in 14 *parallax*, January–March 2000, 13–24.
33. Consider the brilliant staging of the contrast between the Indian and *Latino* woman in terms of make up in Elisabeth Burgos-Debray (ed.) *I, Rigoberta Menchu: an Indian Woman in Guatemala*, trans. A. Wright (London: Verso, 1983) 210.
34. Excerpted from Gayatri Chakravorty Spivak, *In Other Worlds* (London: Routledge, 2006).
35. S. Freud, 'Fetishism', in J. Strachey, et al. trans., *The Standard Edition of the Complete Psychological Works* (New York: Norton, 1964), Vol. XXI, 152–7.

5
Constructing and Deconstructing the Universal: Jacques Derrida's *Sinnliche Gewissheit*

Etienne Balibar

It is an honour to be delivering one of the lectures commemorating the life and work of Jacques Derrida, one of the great contemporary philosophers, in a European country that he visited so many times, and where he has so many friends. I had the privilege of being his student, later his colleague and friend, and I keep learning from him. I want to thank you very sincerely for your invitation. I understood that the purpose of these lectures was to insert Derrida's writings and ideas in the course of a broader argument, in order to show how he has been continuing and recasting fundamental issues in philosophy, with a distinctive style and theoretical orientation. In this spirit, I had suggested the title 'Constructions and Deconstructions of the Universal'. It was my intention to show how Derrida's practice of 'deconstruction' initiated a completely new way of dealing with the classical 'paradoxes of the universal', notably by dismantling the opposition of the universal and the particular.

In the course of my preparation, I was led, understandably, to place special importance on the relationship between deconstruction and the dialectical 'construction' of the universal proposed by Hegel, both in his speculative writings, such as the *Logic*, and in his more 'concrete' investigations, such as the *Elements of the Philosophy of Right*,[1] *Lectures on the Philosophy of World History*,[2] the *Aesthetics*,[3] etc., and inherited by modern philosophy, at least on the 'continental' side. However, while working along these lines, I was led to modify my project and take the risk of offering something both more specific, perhaps limited, and more technical. I hope this will allow us to hear Derrida's written voice in a more effective manner. My talk will be simply a reading of a celebrated passage in the first chapter of Hegel's *Phenomenology of Spirit* entitled, in German, *Phänomenologie des Geistes*.[4] This phrase has been translated as 'la certitude sensible', in French, and as 'sense-certainty', in English. The German term *Gewissheit*, found in many classical contexts, has the meaning of conviction and faith while *sinnlich* means also *sensual* or sensuous. This will be followed by readings of certain passages in Derrida, particularly from *La carte postale* (1980),[5] *Parages* (1986),[6] his 1993 trilogy, *Khôra*, *Passions*, and *Sauf le nom*,[7] and from *Le monolinguisme de l'autre* (1996).[8] I will try to demonstrate that these texts taken together form what we might call Derrida's 'sense certainty' or *sinnliche Gewissheit* in a permanent but also tense and critical relationship to Hegel. In the middle, I will make a detour through an additional text, which I will briefly interpret. This is the essay *'L'appareil formel de l'énonciation'*, by Emile Benveniste, one of the great achievements of Twentieth century French structuralism. The essay was published in 1970 and was later reprinted in 1974 in Volume II of *Problèmes de linguistique générale*[9] (to my knowledge this second volume has not been translated yet into English). It bears a striking relationship with Hegel's chapter and provides some necessary clues for understanding Derrida's analysis of language, thus forming the intermediary link between Derrida and Hegel.

One reason for embarking on this series of textual readings is that they contain some fundamental elements for understanding the theme of universality in contemporary philosophy and, especially, in the so-called 'deconstructive' approach. It is widely accepted that Hegel's dialectic of sense certainty deals very little (if at all) with the question of the 'senses'. Its main theme is the paradoxical effects of the 'personal pronoun' *Ich* (*I* or *Je*) and of the indexical designators *Dieser* and *Dieses*, *Hier* and *Jetzt* (*this* and *that*, *here* and *now*). The chapter contains, at least negatively, the preliminary step for an explanation of the relationship between the categories of the singular and the universal, suggesting that this relationship is not so much a logical opposition but a reversible unity, with each of its terms being the reverse side of the other. I hope to be able to show that Derrida pushes this founding paradox of universality to the extreme, in a sense making it unsurpassable but also filling it with a wealth of literary, ethical and political elements which give it an extraordinary phenomenological relevance.

A consequence and a subsequent reason for my somewhat ascetic choice is that I want to illustrate, through these comparative readings, the intimate and intricate reciprocity that has developed recently between the dialectical tradition, the structuralist revolution and the post-modernist reform of philosophy, for which the names of Hegel, Benveniste and Derrida can be considered as emblematic. The relationship between these currents and schools is anything but external, if only because they permanently return to the same examples or situations. This can be shown however only if we enter the discipline of textual reading, leaving aside the abstract comparisons of doctrines and opinions.

This brings me to the last, the main reason perhaps for addressing you in this manner. As I was re-reading books and drafting formulations around the problem of universality, I felt a growing and eventually irrepressible desire to discuss the issue not at a general level and *in abstracto*, but in a textual mode, retracing the adventures of writing, as an intellectual experience whose results are always unpredictable. I became aware that the source of this desire was not only that I found it absurd to transform Derrida' formulations on universality and singularity into a doctrine or a system, in the sense in which there is a Hegelian system, and possibly also a structuralist system (although the nearly tautological character of this formulation should warn us that it covers a difficulty). Additionally, Derrida's philosophical practice of writing, his distinctive 'style' in philosophy if you like, which has drawn so many contradictory and equally passionate reactions of admiration and rejection, is not purely reducible to his formal 'concept' of writing. It calls for a special kind of commentary made up not of analytic or synthetic reductions to an ideal content, a commentary that *reiterates* the material process of writing. Derrida constantly practised a type of writing *in the margins of other texts* or between their lines, 'supplementing', as it were, their original enunciations in order to manifest their virtualities, their direct or inverted uses. Such a commentary would therefore expand the range of efficiency of Derrida's deconstructive moves to new contexts including his own work. Derrida maintained, to the surprise and even disagreement of some readers, that deconstruction should deconstruct everything except itself. But I am convinced that, in his view, this would not imply that his own texts should stay immune or untouchable.

After theses precautions, let us move to our texts. First, allow me to read, just read, a passage from *Le monolinguisme de l'autre* (*Monolingualism of the Other*). I will read it in French, because I had only the French version while preparing this lecture. I will not provide a translation however because I believe that certain effects and qualities of writing can only be perceived in the original language (provided, perhaps, they are explained in another). You may remember that the general theme of Derrida's book (which I consider one of his most remarkable, because of the way it combines autobiography and theory) is the paradox of a man – himself. But we are asked to consider his case as paradigmatic of the relationship of all speaking subjects to their 'mother-tongue'. A man can speak and write precisely and fully one language only, have it as *his* language, in the sense of acknowledging and identifying with it (in the case of Derrida, French), even when he speaks or writes in another tongue, while maintaining that, in the last instance, this language is not *his own*, but the language of the *other*: 'Quiconque doit pouvoir déclarer sous serment, dès lors: je n'ai qu'une langue et ce n'est pas la mienne, ma langue "propre" m'est une langue inassimilable. Ma langue, la seule que je m'entende parler et m'entende à parler, c'est la langue de l'autre.'[10] [Editor's note: The original French is kept throughout the text as it was Balibar's wish. Translations in English are provided in the endnotes.]

Who is this Other? In the case of a French-Algerian Jew, the Other is the master, the coloniser. But this *master*, in turn, does not really *own* his language, because this language is haunted, permeated, by the repressed presence of the languages of the colonised and is therefore incompatible with the representation of absolute mastery; finally, because *all language* for any speaker or group of speakers is permanently transformed by its more or less violent contact with others and escapes every possible identification with a natural or historical *property* of that community. In the following passage, Derrida is reflecting on the value of his testimony about the violent element of dispossession inherent in his relation to his own alienated and alienating mother tongue. He therefore speaks in the first person:

Que se passe-t-il quand quelqu'un en vient à décrire une 'situation' prétendument singulière, la mienne par exemple, à la décrire en en témoignant dans des termes qui le dépassent, dans un langage dont la généralité prend une valeur en quelque sorte structurelle, universelle, transcendantale ou ontologique? Quand le premier venu sous-entend: 'Ce qui vaut pour moi, irremplaçablement, cela vaut pour tous.' La substitution est en cours, elle a déjà opéré, chacun peut dire, pour soi et de soi, la même chose. Il suffit de m'entendre, je suis l'otage universel.[11]

This is what I will call Derrida's 'sense certainty', his *sinnliche Gewissheit*. At this point, I would like to embark on a long detour, which will take us back, first, to Hegel's *Phenomenology of Spirit*, published in 1807.

Hegel's chapter is very strange. It is short, just ten pages in most editions and translations. It supposedly solves the riddle of the *beginning* of a dialectical process which, in its principle, rejects the idea of any fixed or substantial starting point, any 'prerequisite' that would be posited artificially by virtue of its empirical evidence or its alleged rational self-sufficient character. In this sense, it is related to a sceptical move without which the very idea of dialectics would be meaningless. Every time Hegel is confronted with the problem of the beginning, he resolves it by constructing an initial paradox, positing not a single term but a unity of contradictory notions whose tension will initiate an infinite process of development, a succession of increasingly more concrete and complete figures. In the *Logic*, this is the well-known identity of *Sein* and *Nichts*, Being and Nothingness, whose resolution is *Werden*, becoming, the key term of dialectics.[12] In the *Phenomenology*, however, Hegel follows a different and much more complicated path. The 'subject' of the dialectical development is *the subject* itself, or 'consciousness' (which at a certain point will become 'self-consciousness'). A comprehensive notion of consciousness will be properly constructed, involving both an individual and a collective or cultural aspect and featuring a permanent tension between the particular and the universal or, between the more 'subjective' aspect of *certainty* (*Gewissheit*) and the more 'objective' aspect of *truth* (*Wahrheit*). Hegel, in order to start the substantial development but also to set up its motor or driving force (this is throughout this grand narrative the incapacity of consciousness to 'reconcile' its representations of truth or its knowledge of the world with its criteria of certainty), offers a kind of pre-phenomenological description of the phenomena of consciousness, a paradoxical figure of *conscious-ness before consciousness*. In this 'figure', consciousness is reduced to the formal possibility of referring a representation to a subject, *ego* or *I (Ich)*. But this representation – or better perhaps this *presentation* – in turn is not even an 'object'. It has no 'properties', it emerges before the possibility of associating 'properties' with an object to which the properties belong. This possibility will arise only with the next step, called *Wahrnehmung* (perception). The pre-object for the pre-subject called *Ich* is only a *thing*, a *something* referred to as *Dieses* 'that'. In fact this is not a cognitive but an indexical notion, a theoretical equiva-lent for the gesture of showing *(zeigen)*, a verb that recurs several times in the text.

In the middle of the text and after various preliminaries, Hegel argues that the essence of this absolutely elementary correlation between *Ich* and *Dieses*, *I* and *that*, lies in the transitory unity of both terms, which seem distinct but are in reality indiscernible. The unity, however, is bound to remain evanescent, a vanishing gesture if you like. In more recent terminology, it is a pure but completely abstract 'sense-datum' because it precedes every perception in the proper sense. Such a coincidence is best indicated through the use of monosyllabic interjections such as 'here' and 'now', which also play a crucial role in the text. Hegel goes on to show that this vanishing unity immediately falls into separated aspects or terms: the *I* and the *that*. This is a subtle point, because, in reality, the separation is an illusion. *I* am nothing different from what I indicate, and that some-thing I indicate is nothing else from the intention of my gesture (this is one of the possible meanings of the term *Meinen*, which constantly plays on the proximity with *Mein*, 'my' or what is 'mine'). What gives these terms a seeming autonomy is a characteristic that adds to the paradoxical character of the 'experience' described. It is the fact that each term immediately appears in a contradictory manner as purely singular and completely universal (and for that reason unsustainable for the consciousness, whose emergence Hegel is describing). *I am myself*, or I am *myself*, nothing else, nobody else, designating this thing there, at this moment, no more. But *I* could be anybody, the *I* is open to an infinite range of substitutions, it is universal. Similarly, *this is this thing*, here and now, but *here is anywhere* and *now is any time*, so that the same infinite range of substitutions, the same universal quality characterises also the 'objective' side of the sense-certainty.

I have summarised the idea of the sense-certainty and recalled how it confronts us with the simple and radical formulation of the indiscernibility of the singular and the universal, when they are attributed to pure figures of designation. We can proceed now to the heart of the matter, which has to do with the *writing of the text*. To be sure, Hegel's representation of the origin of dialectics in the *Phenomenology*, anticipating proper consciousness (and also, for that reason, an overcoming of consciousness, the fact that consciousness is not the whole, the final word of mental or spiritual activity), is not entirely unprecedented.[13] This is historically important but it is not Hegel's most original contribution. More significant, perhaps, is Hegel's harsh critique of a certain notion of the 'unspeakable', 'unsayable', or *'inexpressible'* (*das Unaussprechliche*) at the end of the chapter, because it draws our attention to the importance of language. This notion belongs both to the most ancient mystical tradition and the more recent romantic philosophy of religion. It suggests that the alleged inexpressible in fact expresses only a contradiction, it designates a singularity that has no content or determination, a singularity indiscernible from pure generality. Hegel is able to raise this critique only because, right from the beginning, the dialectic of sense-certainty has been presented at the level of discourse, more precisely, in the form of enunciating or saying. The experience called 'sense-certainty' has nothing to do with perception or with sensation in the psychological or physiological sense. It is a pure linguistic experiment and the contradiction to which it directs our attention is not that of empirical consciousness, but a contradiction in the use of language that structures and *precedes* our experiences. This is all the more remarkable because, after this beginning, Hegel apparently drops the reference to language as a constitutive aspect of consciousness and re-introduces it at a much later stage, when consciousness appears as a cultural process. This follows the fact that the language alluded to in the first chapter is absolutely elementary – reduced to a few words and one function, designation and self-designation. Better put, it is an arch-language, what I will dare to call *writing* in Derrida's sense.[14]

But how could such a language be presented, how could its logical function and its effects become perceived? There is only one way to do it and at this point Hegel's text becomes fantastic: the abstract generic terms of the sense-certainty, the *I* and the *That* express their position themselves, they *speak* (the German text uses both *sprechen* and *sagen*) through a kind of *theoretical ventriloquy*. Hegel's narrative on sense-certainty, a short narrative before the grand narrative of consciousness where the abstractions are attributed to language, is in a sense fantastic but certainly not arbitrary. Because the subject and the object must speak and words must be uttered, the contradictory unity of the singular and the universal must emerge, in an indisputable manner, as an effect of experience itself. I say *I* and *I* is already *another*. This is either because I am no longer the same 'I', I am changing, I have already changed; or, because some other subject has taken my place and speaks, in turn, with exactly the same right and the same certainty. I say *this* and it is already *that*, which is different. I say *here* and it is *elsewhere*. I say *now* and it is *later*. I repeat, for example, 'day' and it is 'night', 'tree' and it is 'house'. The same words – *I, this, here, now* – which provide experience with its elementary structure, display also the contradiction at the heart of that experience. They do not express pre-existing subjects or beings but are pure functions of language, which become punctually realised or instantiated in the vanishing of experience. Hegel comes as close as possible to introducing the category of 'performative contradiction' – perhaps he does not use the term or some equivalent, only because he wants the contradiction to become formulated from inside its experience. He writes *as if* 'I' were displaying myself in the contradictory nature of my *speech act*, in a reflexive manner. I name myself as myself, the same self, with the pronoun *I* and the form of my statement contradicts its reference, because I am always already *other*. The same applies in relation to the thing, something, anything. The combination of the fiction of ventriloquy, the practical use of the logical categories of self-referential meaning and the paradoxes of the relationship between the act of enunciation and the meaning of the enunciated makes this an extraordinary text, for contemporary readers at least, who know their Benveniste and Derrida. I am sure it *was* already extraordinary when it was written, in its historical and literary context.

Let us move now to the other text I want to read with you in a Derridean manner and let us also trace its influence on Derrida. It is Emile Benveniste's *'L'appareil formel de l'énonciation'*. It is part of a much broader range of essays, most of which are collected in the first volume of *Problèmes de linguistique générale*, in a section under the general title, *L'Homme dans la langue* and, more rigorously from a structuralist point of view, *De la subjectivité dans la langue*, translated as *subjectivity in language*.[15] These texts deal with the meaning and use of personal pronouns, starting with a celebrated definition of what is and is not a 'personal' pronoun. Only *I* and *You* name 'persons' in the linguistic sense. *He*, *She* or *They*, the alleged 'third persons', are *not* 'persons' in the proper sense. They also deal with the relations of tenses in the verbal forms (including a remarkable criterion of distinction between the two fundamental modes of past enunciation that can be called *historical narrative* and *subjective discourse*). Finally, they include a critical discussion of the Austinian notion of the *performative* and its dependence on the qualifications of the speaker and the conditions of realisation of its effects, of 'doing things with words'.

These classical articles were written in the Fifties and early Sixties and are contemporary – to give a point of comparison – with Lévi-Strauss' first great works on *Elementary Structures of Kinship* and on 'structural anthropology'.[16] In the later essay on the formal apparatus of enunciation, I am considering now, Benveniste systematises his theory, which is indiscernibly linguistic and philosophical. He describes the function of personal pronouns, the meaning of tense differences and the efficiency of performatives (such as *je jure, nous jurons, je promets, je décrète – I swear, we swear, I promise, I order that*), as complementary aspects of the process taking place *within language itself,* through the use of pure linguistic instruments and forms. This process allows subjects to *appropriate language*, which means at the same time representing themselves within the linguistic structure, acquiring the disposition of language as a totality and, setting the conditions for a proper use of semantic categories. To be sure, these 'subjects' or 'subjectivities' are very general structural categories. But they are also practically represented or instantiated, by each one of us every time we perform the discursive function they indicate. This is precisely the structuralist transformation of the category of the subject, as encountered in Lévi-Strauss in relation to kinship structures and in Lacan's structure of the unconscious.

Jean-Claude Milner, the French linguist and philosopher, has convincingly argued, in a recent essay,[17] that the discussion of personal pronouns in Benveniste is so directly reminiscent of Hegel's presentation of sense-certainty that it must have been inspired by it. This is especially evident in the way Benveniste correlates the meaning of the indicators *this* and *that*, the adverbs *now* and *here*, and also, strikingly, the assertive and denying interjections, *yes*, and *no*, with the self-referential element determining the meaning of personal pronouns. Who is *I*? *I* is purely the person actually speaking, whoever she is, who names herself as the speaker in a certain act of enunciation, or speech act, whereas *You* is purely the person addressed by the person who refers to herself as the speaker. This is what Benveniste calls a 'correlation of subjectivity'.[18] Milner's argument about the continuities between structuralism and a certain dialectical tradition gives a convincing and probably original reading of that tradition. But it is not sufficient for my purposes.

I will continue the reading in a more complex way. I will try to indicate what Derrida must have drawn from Benveniste, albeit in a subversive manner, reversing and challenging the meaning of one of Benveniste's most crucial claims. On the basis of that critical comparison, I will return to Hegel's idea of sense-certainty, to show that it can be read as directly 'self-deconstructing'. I have invented or rather guessed this reading of Benveniste by Derrida, but I am not taking great risks. Derrida's published works have frequent references to Benveniste, either in themselves or combined with references to other theorists such as Lévi-Strauss (in *Given Time* for example).[19] These are often very critical. But to my knowledge, there is no reference to this passage in Benveniste, which is the most important if we are to understand Derrida's relation to structural linguistics. I must therefore reconstruct the debate.

At the beginning of his essay, Benveniste defines 'enunciation' as a *grand procès*, a 'great process', in which a speaker sets language in motion for his own purpose (in French, language here is *'la langue'*, one of two possible terms, as is *Sprache*, in German). Benveniste adds that enunciation is a working (*fonctionnement*) of language through an individual *act* or *action of use*, insisting on 'action' as much as on 'use'; it is an active 'conversion' of language into individual discourse or utterance. This process has different aspects, but Benveniste wants to focus on the formal framework (*'cadre formel'*) of the process, the formal conditions of what is essentially an individual action. In the course of the explanation, it becomes clear that these are transcendental *a priori* conditions for the constitution of subjectivity in and through language. The first group of conditions, which determines the mechanism of reference to a world of objects and allows entry into the process of *appropriation* of meaning, concerns the introduction of the speaker into his own discourse, or the 'presence' of the speaker 'to' his own enunciation. They depend entirely on the fact that a speaker can speak in the first person and in the present tense. This is indeed very close to the Hegelian description of the correlation between *I* and *this* or *that, here* and *now*, with some additional technical specifications. Immediately, however, Benveniste proposes a crucial rectification. Whereas Hegel's ventriloquist 'speaker', 'sense-certainty' or consciousness before consciousness, was a solipsistic if not a narcissistic figure, entirely contained in the use of the *I*, Benveniste's speaker is dual and dialogic. It has two names, *I* and *you*, which means that meaningful speaking can only take place in the form of a dialogue with an interlocutor (*allocutaire*) however complex or imaginary. Better put, this is an *anticipated* dialogue in which a subject addresses a possible interlocutor, indeed the simple *possibility* of an interlocutor. These twin names are constantly *relived, re-born or newly*-born: 'Ils sont engendrés chaque fois qu'une énonciation est proférée, et chaque fois ils désignent à neuf.'[20]

One could say, although this is not Benveniste's terminology, that the process of appropriation, the introduction of subjectivity in language without which language remains an abstraction, takes the form of a process of communication, a 'commerce' or an 'intercourse' in the classical sense. This intercourse is symmetrical. The positions of *I* and *You* can be exchanged, and *must be exchanged* at some point. To put it differently, the subjective appropriation of language exists only as a social process and produces not an individual but a trans-individual subject. This does not make however the two subject-positions and the two pronouns interchangeable. On reflection, it becomes apparent that what Benveniste calls a *personal pronoun* in the transcendental sense is not the *I* or *You* separately but the dialogic correlation of subjectivities, the *coupling* of I and You. This is the reason why *He* or *She* are not *personal* pronouns, but impersonal designators with the same status as *this, that* or *it* in languages which have a neutral. The true personal pronoun is dialogic, the coupling itself, but you have to read it in an oriented way. Interestingly, in his first formulations, Benveniste tends to give a privilege to the *I* over the *You*, somewhat weakening the subjective character of the correlation. When the speaker 'signals his position' in discourse through the use of *I*, he *provokes*, at least potentially, a *reaction* from an interlocutor. But later, he reverses the primacy of the *I*, the first agent, into a quasi-primacy of the *You*, so that a speaker can enter language only because he or she is *anticipating* or *imagining* a reply from his or her interlocutor, however deferred and oblique that reply may be.

A Lacanian interpretation of this description would amount to the famous saying according to which the subject receives his or her message from the Other in an inverted form. It would insist that every speech act, unconsciously, repeats a primordial experience in which the subject has been interpellated, called by his or her name, whichever name, such as 'my little thing', or 'my darling', or 'you monster', etc., by some Big Other (Father or Mother). But the Derridean reading, I propose, is quite different. It insists that 'the letter can also not reach its addressee'. If it is to be a universal, open to every possibility and every *event*, leaving no exception, it ought never to reach the addressee or provoke his reaction in the form of an answer. The decisive fact in communication is not only that it can be established, but that it can be broken, that it can or even *must fail*, that a perfect or adequate answer, especially to a question or a calling, is indeed impossible. Echoing another well-known deconstructive reading of metaphysical dualities, we might say that the answer is indefinitely postponed, 'deferred', it displays a *différance*. It does not concentrate in the dialogic symmetry of persons but is 'disseminated', escaping their grip, remaining out of reach and exposed to *loss*.

This is especially notable, almost painfully tangible, in the literary status of certain callings, particularly the calling *viens*, 'come', improperly called an imperative in our grammar textbooks. Derrida emphasises the primacy of the absent or impossible Other over its *presence*, even when somebody *is there*, perhaps especially when somebody *is there* who will not do, will not respond perfectly, but who is still called by the quasi-name *You*. In this sense, the *You* tends to become, not the name of an actually *present* Other (the interlocutor), or a potentially present Other (in the sense of a possibility that could be realised) but of an Other whose 'certainty' remains forever problematic, whose full presence is equated with *the impossible*.

It is especially in his commentaries of Blanchot's novels that Derrida has insisted on this idea, or rather has implemented it in his own writing, as in this passage from *Parages*:

Viens. Viens: comment appeler ce que je viens de – ce que je viens
de quoi. Ce que je viens de dire? Viens, est-ce un mot? Un mot de
la langue française? Un verbe? Voilà en apparence un impératif
nécessairement présent, mode ici conjugué à la deuxième per-
sonne du singulier. Cette définition paraît aussi sûre qu'insuffi-
sante…Qu'ai-je fait? J'ai appelé. Comment appeler *cela?* As-tu
remarqué comment cela, 'Viens', disons ce mot étrange, dans
L'arrêt de mort, tout près de la fin, avant ces deux derniers para-
graphes disparus d'une édition à l'autre et provoquant plus, par
leur disparition…Je dois vous interrompre, vous me perdez.
M'avez-vous dit 'viens' ou déjà cessé de me parler pour vous
entretenir, vous, avec qui que ce soit, de ce è disons ce mot, et de
savoir comment il – il quoi, au fait? Je suis perdue…'[21]

In *Demeure*, another book on Blanchot written after his death,
(whose title is a name, but also a calling, with a play on words,
meaning both 'home' or 'mansion' and 'stay' or 'please, stay', the
reverse of 'come', *viens!* – perhaps, even, keep coming while you are
already there), Derrida formulates the logical conclusion, *'Je devient
Tu'*,[22] I becomes You. I would paraphrase this as the new sense-
certainty, in which the *I*, the founding reference, is not *I* but *You*,
the elusive and impossible addressee.

What is even more impressive is the way in which the topic of the
subjective correlation and the primacy of the *You* is treated in *La
carte postale. De Socrate à Freud et au-delà.* Philosophers read it mostly
for its appendixes, including the famous critique of Lacan, *'Le facteur
de la vérité',* ('Truth's Postman'). You recall that the first and longest
part of the book is a fictional and enigmatic love correspondence
(is there an autobiographic element behind that?) dealing with the
strange discovery of an ancient postcard at the Bodleian Library in
Oxford where Plato is shown looking at a writing Socrates from
behind. The fact that a philosophical concept emerges in the course
of a fiction, especially a fictitious correspondence, should not surprise any reader of Rousseau's *Nouvelle Héloïse.* Allow me to read one
short passage, from the letter dated 5 June 1977:

Tu me donnes les mots, tu les délivres, un à un dispensés, les
miens, en les tournant vers toi et te les adressant – et je ne les ai
jamais tant aimés, les plus communs devenus très rares, ni tant

aimé les perdre non plus, les détruire d'oubli à l'instant même où tu les reçois, et cet instant précéderait presque tout, mon envoi, moi-même, les détruire d'oubli, avant moi, pour qu'ils n'aient lieu qu'une fois. Une seule fois, tu vois la folie pour un mot? Ou pour quelque trait que ce soit?[23]

Tu me donnes les mots: *You* give me the words, it is you who gives me the words, it is the *You* which gives the reality of 'language' to the *I*, rather than the *I* being the origin or the master of his own language.

But something more emerges here, totally absent from Benveniste's 'formal apparatus of enunciation', even though it derives entirely from its formalism. Something that *should have been* considered by Benveniste as a constitutive or quasi-transcendental feature of the 'great process' of dialogic appropriation of language. The fact that it was neglected by this great linguist may lead us to think that it was *repressed* or tacitly denied. It is not simply the sexualised or gendered character of a purely imaginary communication. It is more cogent and 'real' than that: it is the fact that you cannot start an intercourse with the pronouns *I* and *You* without raising the issue of gender, albeit in a paradoxical manner, evoking and neutralising it at the same time, deferring it, making it somehow undecidable. There is an *erotic* but also an *enigmatic*, disturbing element, a 'gender trouble' in every real correspondence, which comes from the fact that correspondents are necessarily either of the same sex or, of different sex. But language immediately covers the problem that it itself raised.

Hear again the passage, I just read, from *La carte postale*; read all the others. A perceptible and compelling sexual difference enters the use of the *I* and *You*, but which exactly? We read Jacques Derrida, a man's name on the front page and this 'proper' name is echoed in the text by allusions to 'his' works. This way we easily fall into the trap of imagining that the *I* who writes the letters about Socrates and Plato represents the author himself, always forgetting the simplest lesson of literature: 'Madame Bovary c'est moi', etc. We tend to imagine that the *I* in the text is a male character, the addressee a female. But this is precisely what language forbids. I once asked a friend of mine, a learned linguist but not a declared feminist, whether there exist languages in which the personal pronouns are gendered, as they are numbered, distinguishing the male from the female speaker as they distinguish the single from a collective speaker. 'Oh no!', she replied, 'there must remain a universal element in language.' But this element is permanently denied in the very *use*, the *mobilisation*, of linguistic forms. The universal is silently invaded by the singular, in the form of the persisting question of sexual *difference or indifference* within the neutral dialogic apparatus. It is perhaps its necessary silence, its *unspeakable element*.

I am tempted to add that this is the obscure side of Benveniste's famous thesis that only *I* and *You*, or *You* and *I*, are personal pronouns, whereas *He* and *She* are not. This is indisputably the case in relation to the description of the formal relationship between the act of enunciation and the words in discourse. But it also indicates that the 'correlation of subjectivity' represses and denies the expression of sexual difference or indifference in terms of linguistic genders. Or, perhaps, we should say, again, that the expression is only postponed, deferred, it arrives when a third person enters discourse. At some point it will be *provoked*. The third person, a false or improper person, is as necessarily gendered, with all the possible equivocations, as the first and the second persons are necessarily neutral. There is no language, no appropriation of language, without third persons, just as there is no language and no use of it without first and second persons.

This may be the reason why Derrida has coined the complex and somewhat barbaric neologism 'ex-appropriation', which combines in an oxymoronic manner the ideas of appropriation and being expropriated. When you appropriate language by speaking in the first person in the present tense (Benveniste is quite right to explain that this is not a partial, piecemeal and progressive acquisition but a sudden and total *event*) you are in fact appropriating *nothing* that you can call 'mine' or 'yours'. Better still you irreversibly lose something after which you were running, namely your *identity*. So perhaps there is a 'subject' within and of language, but this subject is hopelessly deprived of a fixed and recognisable identity. Unfortunately. Or, fortunately.

We have now reached a decisive point in the process of deconstruction of the idea of subjectivity as a function of the structure of communication using the privileged example of Benveniste. We see clearly that a deconstruction is not a destruction, a final overcoming or a way of putting aside the universalistic categories of metaphysics. On the contrary, it is a way of expressing the intrinsic tensions and limits associated with what they suppress from representation, only to see it emerging again in the form of a remainder, a supplement, a deferral. We come very close to the idea that, indeed, every great metaphysical theory, be it that of Rousseau, Plato, Hegel, or Benveniste, 'self-deconstructs' or can be deconstructed only from the inside, albeit with the help of the *strange*, the *foreign* element it represses.

I could stop here, because this is already an interesting result. But if you allow me, I will try to generalise and return to my starting point, Hegel's model of sense-certainty or *sinnliche Gewissheit* and the general theme of the construction of the universal.

On returning to Hegel after Benveniste and, especially, after reading Benveniste in a Derridean deconstructive mode, it is clear that Hegel not only made use of linguistic forms but moreover invented a formalisation of linguistic forms in order to show that the singular and the universal are indiscernible at the level of enunciation. Hegel created a figure, a schematism of linguistic 'space', which is both elusive and compelling. This is not exactly the space of communication, although it involves a latent notion of communication and interpellation haunting Hegel's figure of ventriloquy. The sense-certainty, this volatile unity of self and other indicated by such exclamations as 'here is tree', 'here is house', 'now is day', 'now is night', has been given a voice: it *speaks*, *es spricht, elle parle ou ça parle*. But *to whom* does it speak? To *itself* or to another sense-certainty, a rival figure, or more likely to 'us', the enigmatic name constantly used by Hegel to bring into the text the critical agency drawing the lessons from the various dialectical conflicts and contradictions in the successive figures of consciousness. We may suspect that this philosophical 'We' is itself also a kind of ventriloquist figure, a voice from inside, a voice without a voice haunting the same space, the same multiplicity of Words and Phrases. In short, this linguistic space preceding the consciousness of language and making it possible is neither material nor ideal, it is rather *spectral*. It has the same characteristics as those other 'spectral spaces' Derrida uncovered and described in his work, from the early space of archwriting, the *texte* without any *hors texte*, woven of an infinity of traces, to the *Khôra* taken from Plato's *Timaeus*, in the essay of the

same name, the space of 'places' before their distinction and fixation, before topology and geometry, a space of writing and speaking,
organised this time around another disturbing relation, that of pronouns and proper names. A space that creates the possibility for a
certain kind of discourse, call it philosophy if you like, to escape clas-
sifications and appropriations in the public sphere. Derrida wrote, in
Khôra:

> Bien que le nom soit déjà prononcé (*Timée*, 19a), la question de
> *khôra* comme lieu général ou réceptacle total (*pandekhès*) n'est
> certes pas encore posée. Mais si elle n'est pas posée comme telle,
> elle fait signe et pointe déjà. La note est donnée. Car, d'une part,
> la polysémie ordonnée du mot comporte toujours le sens de lieu
> politique ou plus généralement de lieu *investi*, par opposition à
> l'espace abstrait. *Khôra* 'veut dire': place occupée par quelqu'un,
> pays, lieu habité, siège marqué, rang, poste, position assignée, ter-
> ritoire ou région. Et de fait, *khôra* sera toujours déjà occupée,
> investie, même comme lieu général, et alors qu'elle se distingue de
> tout ce qui prend place en elle. D'où la difficulté de la traiter
> comme un espace vide ou géométrique, voire, c'est ce qu'en dira
> Heidegger, comme ce qui 'prépare' l'espace cartésien, l'*extensio* de
> la *res extensa*. Mais d'autre part, en ce lieu précis et sur ce lieu
> marqué, le discours de Socrate, sinon le discours socratique,
> procède ou affecte de procéder depuis l'errance, depuis une place
> mobile ou non-marquée, en tout cas depuis un espace d'exclusion
> qui se trouve de surcroît neutralisé. Pourquoi neutralisé? Si Socrate
> feint de se ranger parmi ceux dont le *genre* est de n'avoir pas de
> lieu, il ne s'assimile pas à eux, il dit qu'il leur *ressemble*. Il se tient
> donc dans un troisième genre, en quelque sorte…Sa parole n'est
> ni son adresse ni ce qu'elle adresse. Elle *arrive* dans un troisième
> genre et dans l'espace neutre d'un lieu sans lieu, un lieu où tout se
> marque mais qui serait 'en lui-même' non-marqué.[24]

Later in the same text, we read: 'Cette place introuvable, Socrate ne
l'occupe pas, mais c'est celle depuis laquelle, dans le *Timée* et ailleurs,
il *répond à son nom*. Car il faut toujours, comme *khôra*, "l'appeler de la
même façon". Et comme il n'est pas sûr que Socrate lui-même, celui-
ci, soit quelqu'un ou quelque chose, le *jeu des noms propres* devient
plus abyssal que jamais.'[25] In *Passions*, the companion essay, playing

on the double meaning of *répondre* (response) and *responsabilité* (responsibility) that can also be found in English in the series *to answer, to be answerable*, meaning *responsible for* and, *before X*, Derrida wrote:

> De ce point de vue la responsabilité serait *problématique* dans la mesure supplémentaire où elle pourrait être parfois, peut-être même toujours, celle que l'on prend, non pour soi, *en son propre nom*, et *devant l'autre* (définition métaphysique la plus classique de la responsabilité) mais celle que l'on doit prendre pour un autre, à la place, au nom de l'autre ou de soi comme autre, devant un autre autre, et un autre de l'autre, à savoir l'indéniable même de l'éthique.[26]

We are tempted to suggest that, by means of his critical confrontation with Benveniste, Derrida has given us the possibility to reveal the deconstructive character of Hegel's dialectic or, a possibility of reading it this way. What prevents us from doing so and carrying this suggestion to the end is the fact that, immediately after Hegel had written this astonishing piece of fantastic philosophy, he brutally dropped it and replaced it with the much more rational or perhaps reasonable phenomenology of perception (*Wahrnehmung*). In it, objects do not have names but observable properties and the subject does not speak about itself, but remains a virtual observer. If you take seriously however Hegel's claim that every passage must be justified as a necessary transition arising from the contradictions of the previous figure, this abandonment, this dropping of the figure of language must find an explanation, at least a negative one. Again following indications from Derrida, in *Le monolinguisme de l'autre* and '*Des tours de Babel*', his essay on Benjamin's theory of translation (reprinted in *Psyché*),[27] I would suggest that this may be the case because Hegel simultaneously uses all the resources of language and writing *and* refuses to give them their name, however ambiguous, he refuses to acknowledge their efficient presence in his text. More precisely he refuses to take into account the fact that all the words that he has transformed into quasi-concepts, such as *Ich, Mein, Dieses, Dieser, Hier, Jetzt*, are idiomatic terms, belonging to one (or several) languages, and to very idiomatic uses of these languages which allow the use of puns and verbal associations, such as *mein* and *meinen* (or 'my' and 'meaning'), *Sein* and *sein*, etc. In other words, Hegel does not push the recognition of the paradoxical unity of the universal and the singular where it is perhaps most decisive and coercive, into the domain of language as a universal instrument of communication and a singular (but certainly not particular or private, 'closed') history of forms and meanings, constitutive of subjects but escaping their property, their mastery. Or, perhaps we should even say that he has erroneously confused the problem of the untranslatable, *l'intraduisible*, with that of the *unspeakable, l'indicible ou l'inexprimable, das Unaussprechliche*, and has failed to discuss their intrinsic relation:

> Il faut déjà savoir dans quelle langue *je* se dit, je *me* dis. On pense ici aussi bien au *je pense*, qu'au *je* grammatical ou linguistique, au *moi* ou au *nous* dans leur statut identificatoire, tel que le sculptent des figures culturelles, symboliques, socio-culturelles. De tous les points de vue, qui ne sont pas seulement grammaticaux, logiques, philosophiques, on sait bien que le *je* de l'anamnèse dite autobiographique, le *je-me* du *je me rappelle* se produit et se profère différemment selon les langues. Il ne les précède jamais, il n'est donc pas indépendant de la langue en général. Voilà qui est bien connu mais rarement pris en considération par ceux qui traitent en général de l'autobiographie – que ce genre soit littéraire ou non, qu'on le tienne d'ailleurs pour un genre ou non.[28]

But we might also suggest, in a less arrogant manner, and I take this to be one of Derrida's most precious lessons, that the process of deconstruction is not terminable, therefore continuously includes new discoveries and unpredictable events of interpretation, *hermeneutic events* so to speak. This suggestion becomes inevitable when, on the tracks of dialecticians, structuralists and post-modernists such as Hegel, Benveniste and Derrida, you realise that the alleged conflict, or incompatibility, between universalism and particularism, or absolutism and relativism, is a smokescreen and a children's game for logicians. The really difficult issue lies in *the conflict within universality itself,* or the construction, the production of universals out of their internal inconsistencies.

Notes

1. G. W. F. Hegel, *Elements of the Philosophy of Right*, trans. H. B. Nisbet (Cambridge: Cambridge University Press, 1991).
2. G. W. F. Hegel, *Lectures on the Philosophy of World History*, trans. H. B. Nisbet (Cambridge: Cambridge University Press, 1975).
3. G. W. F. Hegel, *Aesthetics: Lectures on Fine Art*, trans. T. M. Knox (Oxford: Clarendon Press, 1975).
4. G. W. F. Hegel, *Phänomenologie des Geistes* (Berlin: Akademie Verlag, 1964) 79–89 [trans. A. V. Miller, *Phenomenology of Spirit* (Oxford: Clarendon Press, 1979) 58–66].
5. J. Derrida, *La Carte postale. De Socrate à Freud et au-delà* (Paris: Flammarion, 1980) [trans. A. Bass, *The Post Card: From Socrates to Freud and Beyond* (Chicago: Chicago University Press, 1987)].
6. J. Derrida, *Parages*, nouv. éd. revue et augmentée (Paris: Galilée, 1986–2003).
7. J. Derrida, *Khôra* (Paris: Galilée, 1993). *Passions* (Paris: Galilée, 1993), and *Sauf le nom* (Paris: Galilée, 1993) [trans. David Wood, John P. Leavey Jr., and Ian McLeod, *On the Name* (Stanford: Stanford University Press, 1995)].
8. J. Derrida, *Le monolinguisme de l'autre, ou la prothèse de l'origine* (Paris: Galilée, 1996) [trans. Patrick Mensah: *Monolingualism of the Other; or, The Prosthesis of Origin* (Stanford, CA: Stanford University Press, 1998)].
9. E. Benveniste, 'L'appareil formel de l'énonciation', in *Problèmes de linguistique générale II* (Paris: Gallimard, 1974) 79–88.
10. Derrida, *Le monolinguisme de l'autre*, 47. English trans.: 'Consequently, anyone should declare under oath: I have only one language and it is not mine; my "own" language, the only one I hear myself speak and agree to speak, is the language of the other', Derrida, *Monolingualism of the Other*, 25.
11. Derrida, *Le monolinguisme de l'autre*, 40. English trans.: 'What happens when someone resorts to describing an allegedly uncommon "situation", mine, for example, by testifying to it in terms that go beyond it, in a language whose generality takes on a value that is in some way structural, universal, transcendental, or ontological? When anybody who happens by infers the following: "What holds for me, irreplaceably, also applies to all." Substitution is in progress; it has already taken effect. Everyone can say the same thing for themselves and of themselves. It suffices to hear me; I am the universal hostage.' Derrida, *Monolingualism of the Other*, 19–20.
12. G. W. F. Hegel, *Science of Logic*, trans. A. V. Miller (London: George Allen & Unwin, 1969) pp. 81–108.
13. It resumes ideas or schemes of thought that were already there in Plato, or more recently in the empiricist philosophy of the eighteenth century. I am particularly thinking of Condillac's allegory of the sensitive (and sensuous) 'statue', coinciding with the smelling or perfume of a rose at

the beginning of *Traité des sensations*. E. B. De Condillac, *Oeuvres philosophiques*, Georges Le Roy (ed.), Vol. 1 (Paris: PUF, 1947–1951) [trans. F. Philip, *Philosophical Writings of Etienne Bonnot, Abbé de Condillac*, Vol. 1 (Hillsdale NJ: Lawrence Erlbaum, 1982–87)].

14. But not a meta-language, for Hegel there is no meta-language.

15. E. Benveniste. *Problèmes de linguistique générale I* (Paris: Gallimard, 1966) 258–66 [trans. M. E. Meek. *Problems of General Linguistics* (Coral Gables, FL: University of Miami Press, 1971) 223–30)].

16. C. Lévi-Strauss, *Les structures élémentaires de la parenté* (Paris: Mouton, 1967) [trans. J. H. Bell, J. R. von Sturmer, and R. Needham (eds) (*The Elementary Structures of Kinship*, London: Eyre & Spottiswoode, 1968)]. C. Lévi-Strauss, *Anthropologie Structurale* (Paris: Librairie Plon, 1958) [trans. C. Jacobson and B. Grundfest-Schöpf, *Structural Anthropology* (Harmondsworth: Penguin, 1977)].

17. J-C. Milner, BENVENISTE II: *Ibat obscurus*, in *Le périple structural. Figures et paradigme* (Paris: Editions du Seuil, 2002) 87–114.

18. It would be also evident in the way in which Benveniste grants an absolute privilege to the present tense, calling it the 'source of time', by indicating that our whole consciousness of time with its different ek-stases, particularly the past and the future, but also more complicated specifications of each of them, entirely rests on the linguistic distinctions between tenses of verbs which, in turn, entirely rest on the fact that the 'present' is the tense expressing the reference of the speaker to the moment when he or she speaks, or better to the pure fact that he or she is now speaking in these very words.

19. J. Derrida, *Donner le temps 1, La Fausse monnaie* (Paris: Galilée, 1991) 103–4 [trans. by P. Kamuf, *Given Time: I. Counterfeit Money* (Chicago: University of Chicago Press, 1992) 78)].

20. Benveniste, 'L'appareil formel de l'énonciation', 79–88.

21. Derrida, *Parages*, 21. Editor's translation: 'Come. Come: How to call what I have come to – what I have come to what? What I have come to say? Come, is it a word? A word of the French language? A verb? Here apparently a necessarily present imperative, a mode here conjugated in the second person singular [current in French]. This definition seems as much certain as insufficient...What have I done? I have called. How to call *that?* Have you remarked how that "Come" may we say this strange word, in [Blanchot's] *Arrêt de Mort*, very near the end, before these two last paragraphs, disappeared from one edition to the other, and provoking so much by their disappearance...I should interrupt you, you are losing me. Have you told me "come", or have you already stopped speaking to entertain yourself, you [*vous*], with whomever it be, of this, may we say this word, and to know how it – what it, by the way? I am lost [*perdue*].'

22. J. Derrida, *Demeure – Maurice Blanchot* (Paris: Galilée, 1998) 130. [trans. E. Rottenberg, *Demeure: Fiction and Testimony* (Stanford: Stanford University Press, 2000) 96)].

23. Derrida, *La carte postale*, p. 17. English trans.: 'You give me the words, you deliver them, dispensed one by one, my own, while turning them toward yourself and addressing them to yourself – and I have never loved them so, the most common ones become quite rare, nor so love to lose them either, to destroy them by forgetting at the very instant when you receive them, and this instant would precede almost everything, my envoi, myself, so that they take place only once. One single time, you see how crazy this is for a word? Or for any trait at all?' Derrida, *The Post Card*, 12.

24. Derrida, *Khôra*, pp. 58–9. English trans.: 'Although the word was already uttered (19a), the question of *khôra* as a general place or total receptacle (*pandekhés*) is, of course, not yet posed. But if it is not posed as such, it gestures and points already. The note is given. For on the one hand, the ordered polysemy of the word always includes the sense of political place or, more generally, of *invested* place, by opposition to abstract space. *Khôra* "means": place occupied by someone, country, inhabited place, marked place, rank, post, assigned position, territory, or region. And in fact, *khôra* will always already be occupied, invested, even as a general place, and even when it is distinguished from everything that takes place in it. Whence the difficulty – we shall come to it – of treating it as an empty or geometric space, or even, and this is what Heidegger will say of it, as that which 'prepares' the Cartesian space, the *extensio* of the *res extensa*. But on the other hand, the discourse of Socrates in this precise place and on this marked place, proceeds from or affects to proceed from erraticism [*depuis l'errance*], from a mobile or nonmarked place, in any case from a space or exclusion which happens to be, into the bargain, neutralized. Why neutralized? If Socrates pretends to include himself among those whose *genus* [*genre*] is to have no place, he does not assimilate himself to them, he says he resembles them. Hence he holds himself in a third genus, in a way...His speech [*parole*] is neither his address neither what it addresses. His speech *occurs* in a third genus and in a neutral place or a place without place, a place where everything is marked but which would be "in itself" unmarked.' Derrida, *On the Name*, 109.

25. Derrida, *Khôra*, p. 63. English trans.: 'Socrates does not *occupy* this undiscoverable place, but it is one from which, in the *Timaeus* and elsewhere, *he answers to his name*. For as *khôra* he must always "be called in the same way". And as it is not certain that Socrates himself, this one here, is someone or something, the play of the proper names becomes more abyssal than ever.' J. Derrida, *On the Name*, 111.

26. Derrida, *Passions*, pp. 27–8. English trans.: 'From this point of view responsibility would be *problematic* to the further [*supplémentaire*] extent that it could sometimes, perhaps even always, be what one takes, not for oneself, *in one's own name* and *before the other* (the most classically metaphysical definition of responsibility) but what one must take for another, in his place, in the name of the other or of oneself as other, before

another other, and an other of the other, namely the very undeniable of ethics.' J. Derrida, *On the Name*, 10–11.

27. J. Derrida, 'Des Tours de Babel', in *Psyché, Inventions de l'autre*, nouv. éd. Augmentée (Paris: Galilée, 1998) [trans. J. F. Graham, 'Tours de Babel', in J. F. Graham (ed.) *Difference in Translation* (Ithaca: Cornell University Press, 1985)].

28. Derrida, *Le Monolinguisme de l'autre*, p. 54. English trans.: 'It is necessary to know already in what language *I* is expressed, and I *am* expressed. Here we are thinking of the *I think*, as well as the grammatical or linguistical *I*, of the *me* [*moi*] or *us* [*nous*] in their identificatory status as it is sculpted by cultural, symbolic, and sociocultural figures. From all viewpoints, which are not just grammatical, logical, or philosophical, it is well known that the *I* of the kind of anamnesis called autobiographical, the I [*je-me*] of *I recall* [*je me rappelle*] is produced and uttered in different ways depending on the language in question. It never precedes them; therefore it is not independent of language in general. That is something well known but rarely taken into consideration by those dealing in general with autobiography – whether this genre is literary or not, whether it is considered, moreover, as a genre or not.' Derrida, *Monolingualism of the Other*, 28–9.

6
Does Democracy Mean Something?

Jacques Rancière

I must start with a preliminary statement about my intervention in a series dedicated to Derrida. I was never a disciple of Derrida or a specialist on his thought. I had no opportunity to discuss philosophical matters with him, since the time when he was my teacher – very long ago. This is why the tribute I will pay to him is not a commentary on his work. What I can do to honour him is to present my own way of dealing with a concept and a problem, which came increasingly at the foreground of his thinking during the Nineties: what is meant by the name of democracy?

In *Politics of Friendship*, Derrida brings up the issue by commenting on the well-known sentence attributed to Pericles and paraphrased in Plato's *Menexenus*: 'the government of the Athenians is a democracy by the name, but it is actually an aristocracy, a government of the best with the approval of the many'.[1] Derrida points to the oddity of this statement.[2] The very rhetoric of 'democratic' government states that this type of governance can be given two opposite names. It is called a democracy but, as a matter of fact, it is an aristocracy. How can we conceive of this 'but', of this disjunction between the name and the thing? We may view it either as a matter of rhetorical and governmental lie or, we may assume that the difference between the name and the 'thing' points to something more radical, an internal difference, which makes democracy something different from all other types of government. This question can define the common ground between Derrida's inquiry into the aporetic structure of democracy and my own into what I prefer to call the democratic paradox.

In order to spell out what I mean by 'democratic paradox', I will start with two contemporary debates dealing with the name and the reality of democracy. The first involves a major disagreement in relation to the American military campaign for spreading democracy in the Middle East. Immediately after the elections in Iraq and the anti-Syrian protests in Lebanon, the cover of *The Economist* was *Democracy stirs in the Middle East*. The self-satisfaction with this stirring of democracy was formulated according to a two-pronged argumentative structure about the difference between name and reality: democracy stirs *though*... or, democracy stirs *but*.

'Democracy stirs *though*' was the argument of certain idealists, for whom democracy is the self-government of the people. This means that it cannot be brought by force to another people. Put in other terms, we can claim that 'democracy stirs', if we take a pragmatist view of democracy and dismiss the utopian view that it is the 'power of the people'. The second argument was that democracy stirs, *but* bringing democracy does not only mean bringing the rule of law, free elections and so on. It means, first, bringing the mess, the chaos of democratic life. As Donald Rumsfeld put it in relation to the looting that followed Saddam's collapse: we brought freedom to the Iraqis and freedom also means the possibility of doing that kind of thing.

The *though* and the *but* arguments add up to a consistent logic, which runs as follows: because democracy is not the idyll of self-government, because it may lead to a mess, democracy can, and perhaps must, be brought from the outside by the weapons of a superpower. A 'superpower' does not simply imply a country endowed with absolute military superiority. It also means the power of mastering the democratic mess.

At this point, the arguments in support of the military campaigns for spreading democracy remind us of older arguments, which were not so enthusiastic about the spreading of democracy. In fact, they repeat and rephrase the two main arguments about the 'crisis' of democracy, made at the Trilateral Conference, some thirty years ago.

According to the Trilateral, democracy stirs in spite of those democratic dreamers who equate it with the self-government of the people. These dreamers are the same kind of characters as those 'value-oriented intellectuals', who were blamed at the Trilateral Conference for nurturing an 'adversary culture' opposed to the pragmatism of 'policy-oriented intellectuals' and for promoting excessive democratic activity challenging leadership and authority.

Democracy stirs, but the mess stirs alongside. Donald Rumsfeld's joke about the looting in Baghdad sounds like a blunt repetition of Samuel Huntington's argument thirty years ago: democracy leads to an increase in demands which put pressure on governments, undermine authority and make individuals and groups resist the necessities of discipline and sacrifice associated with self-rule.

It turns out that the campaign for spreading democracy in new territories brings to the fore the paradox currently understood under the name of 'democracy'. Good 'democratic government' means a form of government which can master the excess threatening good policy. This excess can be named, its name is *democracy*. As stated in *The Crisis of Democracy*,[3] democratic government is threatened by nothing other than democratic life. This threat appears as a perfect double bind. On the one hand, democratic life means the implementation of the idealistic view of 'self-government' by the people. It entails an excess of political activity encroaching on the principles and procedures of good policy, on authority, scientific expertise and pragmatic experience. Good democracy would therefore mean the lowering of political excess. But this lowering of political activity leads to the empowerment of 'private life' or the 'pursuit of happiness' which, in turn, increases aspirations and demands and undermines political authority and civic behaviour. As a result, 'good democracy' means a form of government able to tame the double excess of political commitment and egotistical behaviour inherent in the essence of democratic life. The contemporary 'democratic paradox' could be stated as follows: democracy as a form of social and political life threatens democracy as a form of government and must be repressed by the latter.

If we are to take a step further in understanding this paradox, it may be helpful to have a look at the second debate I mentioned earlier. It is a smaller disagreement but it may help us grasp the stakes of the main debate and the core of the democratic paradox. Just as American soldiers started pushing for democracy in Iraq, a small book was published in France, which presented the problem of 'democracy in the Middle East' in a very different light and eventually undid the homonymy between 'good' and 'bad' democracy. This is Jean-Claude Milner's *Les Penchants criminels de l'Europe démocratique* (*The Criminal Tendencies of Democratic Europe*).[4] Its author has been known for many reasons but mainly for being the most influential thinker of the so-called 'republican' political theory. According to this theory, citizenship is exclusively grounded on the universality of the law, on education and the authority of knowledge. It opposes all forms of multiculturalism or affirmative action and all encroachment by social or cultural difference on authority and universality.

What is the 'crime' of democratic Europe, according to Milner? In the first instance, it consists in pushing for peace in the Middle East, namely for a peaceful settlement of the Israel–Palestinian conflict. Milner argues that this European peace could mean only one thing, the destruction of Israel. European democracy proposed its own version of peace for solving the Palestinian problem. European democratic peace was the result of the Holocaust. Democratic and peaceful Europe and the end to past European wars was made possible after 1945. At that point, Europe was freed, through the Nazi genocide, from the people who were getting in the way of its dream, namely the Jews. As Milner puts it, 'democratic Europe' means in fact the dissolution of politics, whose principle is rule by a limited totality, into a society whose principle is, on the contrary, limitlessness. Modern democracy is the accomplishment of this law of limitlessness, both emblematised and achieved by technology and culminating nowadays in the project of being freed from the laws of sexual division and filiation. This is why modern European democracy had to annihilate, by means of an appropriate technical invention, the people whose principle is that of filiation and transmission.

This argumentation may seem paranoid. It is in keeping however with a whole trend of thought which, for the last twenty years, has asserted that democracy has been the reign of narcissistic 'mass individualism' which undermines the forms of political agency and the very sense of community by making ever-increasing demands and emphasising particularism and communitarianism. In a sense, Milner makes the same point about the limitlessness of needs, aspirations and demands which, stemming from social life, undermine good policy. His novelty is to radicalise the opposition and to present it as a logical one. The logic and mathematics of democracy, as he puts it, oppose all forms of good government. This is why the good government which could master the democratic excess is no longer called democracy by Milner. It is called, strikingly if discreetly, *pastoral* government. This expression refers to Moses and to *The Murder of the Pastor*,[5] another influential book among former leftist intellectuals, written by Benny Levy, a former Maoist leader. Levy stages the pastor as a biblical figure repressed by the tradition of western philosophy and politics. But 'pastoral government' is above all a notion borrowed from Plato. Levy accuses Plato of having been unfaithful to his own conception of the shepherd examined in *The Statesman*. In fact the matter is more complex. Plato, on the one hand, locates pastoral government in a mythical past when the world was guided directly by the hand of a divine shepherd. On the other, however, the pastoral paradigm is still at work in Plato's view of the rule of the guardians elaborated in the *Republic*.

In my view, the reference to the pastoral government reveals clearly the theoretical kernel of the current argument about democracy, both in the American campaign to spread democracy and in the French indictment of its crimes. The contemporary arguments about the double excess of democracy, as the utopia of the self-government of the people opposed to pragmatic policy or, as the anarchic turmoil of individual desires opposed to the discipline of common law, restages the original setting of democracy in Plato. On the one hand, democracy is, for Plato, the strict regime of written law, which cannot be changed. In this form, it looks like a prescription a physician would have written once and for all, irrespective of the disease to be treated. On the other hand, the rigidity of the letter expresses the sheer arbitrariness of the people, in other words, the unrestricted 'freedom' of individuals to act as they like without concern for common discipline. The Platonic argument means that democracy is not a principle of policy but a way of life which resists good policy. Democracy leads to chaos. More radically, democracy is the way of life where everything is put on its head. Book VIII of the *Republic* describes a state in which all natural relations are overturned. In a democratic city, the rulers instead of ruling follow the ruled, the fathers obey their sons, the elders imitate the young. Women and slaves are as 'free' as men and masters. And even the asses in the streets 'hold on their way with the utmost freedom and dignity, bumping into everyone who meets them and do not step aside'.[6]

The whole post-Tocquevillian argument about democracy as a social way of life and the associated dangers of democratic individualism repeat the old Platonic joke about the proud ass. There is something intriguing about the persistent success of the joke. We are told, every day, that we live in the twenty-first century, in the context of big nations-states, a world-market and powerful technologies which have no longer anything to do with those antique little cities of men whose freedom was based on the exclusion of women, slaves and metics. The conclusion is that our 'democracies' have nothing to do with the government of antique democratic villages. If this is accepted, how can we explain the fact that the polemical description of the democratic village made by an anti-democrat in antiquity is still held as the true portrait of the democratic individual in our world of Stock Exchanges, supermarkets and online economies? The paradox suggests that the way in which the description of democratic life sustains the conceptualisation of democracy may be a deception. The turmoil caused by the unflinchingly democratic ass may signify deeper problems. To put it differently, the standard statement of the democratic paradox (democracy is a form of life that the democratic government has to repress) may indicate a more radical paradox, that of politics itself.

The core of the problem is that democracy is neither a form of government nor a form of social life. Democracy is the institution of politics as such. It is the institution of politics as a paradox. It is a paradox because instituting the political would seemingly give an answer to the question, what grounds the power of rule in a community. Democracy gives an answer to this question, but it is an astounding answer: the very ground for the power of ruling is that no ground exists.

This is what Plato allows us to perceive, in a very quick flash, at the beginning of Book III of *The Laws*. This passage did not receive attention from Derrida in his discussion of democracy, as far as I know. In my view, it may help explain the core of the democratic 'aporia' or 'paradox'. Plato lists, in this passage, the necessary qualifications for ruling. He lists six qualifications, predicated first on a natural difference between the rulers and the ruled. It is the power of parents over children, the elders over the young, the masters over slaves, the nobles over villains, the strong over the weak, the learned over the ignorant. These qualifications involve a clear distribution of positions. One can question, as Plato did, what being 'stronger' truly means, but it is undeniable that weak is the opposite of strong. One may debate whether seniority is a sufficient qualification for the exercise of power, but it is an undeniable qualification. It is an objective difference and a form of power already at work in society. These qualifications can function as an *arkhè* for ruling. An *arkhè* is a theoretical principle as well as a temporal beginning. As a principle, it means a clear distribution of positions and capacities, grounding the distribution of power between rulers and ruled. As a beginning, it means that the fact of ruling is anticipated in the disposition to rule and, conversely, evidence of this disposition is given by the fact of its empirical operation.

It looks as if what is required for a successful government is to provide reasons why some take the position of the rulers and others of the ruled. The first six principles of ruling meet the requirements. But there is a seventh; Plato calls it the 'drawing of lots'.[7] This is democracy, the regime which does not meet the two requirements. Democracy is neither a pre-empted distribution of roles nor the attribution of the exercise of power to a disposition for ruling. The 'drawing of lots' presents the paradox of a qualification which amounts to the absence of all *arkhè*, to a 'qualification without qualification'. Two different consequences may be drawn from this. One may conclude that this qualification is no *arkhè* and drop it from the list of the principles of government. Plato did not follow that route although we cannot accuse him of indulgence toward democracy. This is not only because democracy exists and its 'subject', the people, attests to its existence. There is something more. The democratic lack of *arkhè* backfires on the 'good' qualifications, those which display the appropriate *arkhè*. Good qualifications, indeed. What are they good for exactly? The seniority of the seniors can certainly ground a government. Its precise name would be *gerontocracy*. The knowledge of the learned can ground a government, the name of which could be *epistemocracy* or a *technocracy* and so on and so forth. But *political* government would be missing from that list of governmental forms. If political government means something, it should be something more, superadded to these governments of seniority, fatherhood, science, strength, etc. These forms exist already in families, tribes, schools or workshops and provide patterns for wider and more complex forms of human community. Additionally, there should be something more, coming from Heaven, as Plato puts it. Only two governments come from Heaven. The first is the pastoral, the government of mythical times, when the divine shepherd directly ruled the human flock. The second is the government of chance, the drawing of lots, namely democracy.

Let us put it somewhat differently. There are many patterns of government by means of which men are ruled. The most common are based on birth, wealth, force and science. But politics means something more, a supplementary qualification, common to both the rulers and the ruled. If the divine shepherd no longer rules the world, only one additional qualification exists. This is the qualification of the people who have no greater qualification for ruling than for being ruled. This is the meaning of democracy. The 'power of the demos' is the power of those no *arkhè* entitles to exercise it. Democracy is not a definite set of institutions, nor is it the power of a specific group. It is the supplementary, grounding power, which both legitimises and de-legitimises every set of institutions and the power of any one group of people.

This is the reason for the discomfort the proud ass causes. What gets in the way of good policy is not an excess of demands emanating from so-called mass democracy and individualism but democracy's own ground. The political rests on the supplementary 'power of the people', which both founds it and withdraws its foundations. This coincidence of the grounding and the destroying power is, in my view, more radical that the Derridean concept of democracy's 'auto-immunity'. This auto-immunity has two aspects. It means, first, the unlimited self-criticism inherent in democracy, a capacity, which can empower anti-democratic propaganda. Secondly, it means the possibility that democratic governments may restrict or suspend democratic rights in order to protect democracy from its enemies who use democratic freedoms to fight against it. In both cases, democracy still clings, in Derrida's view, to the unexamined power of the *autos* or *self.* What democracy lacks is otherness, which must come from the outside. This is why Derrida sets out to break the circle of the *self* by weaving a thread from the pure receptivity of the *khôra* through to the *other* or the *newcomer,* whose inclusion demarcates the horizon of a 'democracy to come'.

My objection is very simple. Otherness must not come to politics from outside. Politics has its own otherness, its own principle of heterogeneity. Democracy is precisely this principle. Democracy is not the power of a *self*; on the contrary, it is the disruption of any such power. Democracy means the disruption of the circularity of the *arkhè*. If politics is to exist at all, this anarchical principle must be presupposed. This principle precludes the self-grounding of politics and turns it into the site of division. I tentatively conceptualised that division in the disjunctive relation of three terms: police, politics and the political.

There are men who rule others because they are – or, more accurately, because they play the part of – the elder, the wiser, the richer, etc. There are patterns and procedures of ruling predicated on such and such distribution of qualifications, places and competences. This is what I call the logic of *police*. But if the power of the elders is to be more than a *gerontocracy*; if the learned have to rule not only over the ignorant but also over the rich and the poor; if the ignorant must 'know' what the learned command them to do; if the soldiers have to obey the rulers instead of taking advantage of their weapons for themselves, etc., then the power of the rulers must rely on a supplementary quality common to both rulers and ruled. Power must turn into *political* power.

The logic of police must be thwarted therefore by another logic, that of politics. *Politics* means the supplementation of all qualifications by the power of the unqualified. The reason why the rulers govern is that no good reason exists why some men should rule others. The practice of ruling ultimately rests on its own absence of reason. The 'power of the people' legitimises and de-legitimises it at the same time.

The *demos* in democracy is not the population, the majority of the population, the political body, the low classes, etc. It is the surplus community comprised of those who have no qualification for ruling, which means at once everybody and whoever. The 'power of the people' cannot be equated with the power of any group or institution. It exists only in the form of a disjunction. On the one hand, it is the inner difference which both legitimises and de-legitimises state institutions and practices of ruling. As such, it is a vanishing difference continuously thwarted by the oligarchic running of those institutions. On the other hand, this is why the power of the people must ceaselessly be re-enacted by the action of political subjects who challenge the police distribution of parts, places or competences and restage the anarchical foundation of the political. This disjunction is not an *aporia* but a dissensus. What is *aporetic* is the attempt to ground the political on its own principle. But the foundation is split. Democracy is the practice of dissensus, which keeps re-opening the gap that the practice of ruling relentlessly plugs.

I said earlier that democracy does not consist in a set of institutions. The same laws, the same constitutions can be implemented in opposite ways, depending on the sense of commonality within which they are framed. They can circumscribe the sphere of the political and restrict political agency to an activity performed by definite agents endowed with the appropriate qualifications. Or, they can give way to a democratic interpretation and practice, which invents out of the same texts new political places, issues and agents. What makes the difference is not a set of institutions. It is another distribution of the sensible, another setting of the stage, different relations between words and the kinds of things they designate or the practices they empower. The logic of police consists in circumscribing the sphere of the political. But this shrinking of the stage is usually practised in the name of the purity of the political, the universality of the law or the distinction between political universality and social particularity. Such a 'purification' of politics amounts, in fact, to its dismissal. The democratic logic consists, on the contrary, in blurring and displacing the borders of the political. This is what politics means: displacing the limits of the political by re-enacting the equality of anybody with everybody else as the vanishing condition of the political.

Needless to say that those who want the government of cities and states to be grounded on one simple and unequivocal principle of community find this practice unacceptable. This is the reason for the relentless denunciation of the double bind, duplicity or lie of democracy and for the persistent attempt, from Plato to Samuel Huntington, to prove that its reality contradicts its name. The best-known formulation of this denunciation is found in the opposition between *real* and *formal* democracy. This opposition was strongly emphasised by the Marxist tradition, but it goes far back to the Platonic distinction between democracy as the rule of written law and democracy as a form of individual and social life. There are differences too. In the

Platonic model, the individualistic life of the democrats is the real content of the fake commitment to the rigour of the law. In the Marxist tradition, real democracy is opposed to formal bourgeois democracy, which covers up its dark side, that is the 'real life' of exploitation and inequality. But, while the conclusion is different, the structure of the argument is the same. Formal democracy is the appearance of equality opposed to the reality of inequality. That 'reality' may assume various forms. According to Plato, it may be the sheer pleasure of the democratic individual, subjected to a calculus of pleasure and pain. According to Marx, it may be the reality of private property and interests. The terms may even be reversed, as Hannah Arendt did, by extolling the brightness of the political sphere of appearance against the 'dark background of mere givenness'.

In all these cases, democracy is approached through the filter of the opposition between appearance and reality. It is described, disguised and ultimately dismissed through that opposition. The most telling example of the equivalence of seemingly opposite interpretations can be found in the critique of the revolutionary *'Droits de l'homme et citoyen'*. Nowadays those revolutionary rights have evolved into 'human rights'. We have human rights because authors as diverse as Burke, Marx and Arendt have showed, over two centuries, that there was something wrong about those rights, namely their duplicity. Having two separate subjects is too much, some fallacy must have crept in. This argument has been made by all those authors and was recently resumed by Giorgio Agamben in *Homo sacer*.[8] As Marx put it, the rights of the citizen are in fact the rights of a 'man' who turns out to be the property owner. For Burke and Arendt, these rights present us with a dilemma. They are either the rights of the citizen or those of man. But the rights of man are the rights of the apolitical individual. As this individual has no rights of his own, they are the rights of those who have no rights, which amounts to nothing. Alternatively, the rights of man are the rights of citizens, the rights they possess on account of their belonging to an existing constitutional state. They are the rights of those who have rights, something which amounts to a tautology.

The core of the argument is that if this discourse presents us with two subjects, one of them must be fake. It presupposes that the political subject must be one and the same. The 'true' subject must be either the Man or the Citizen. Politics is either a mirage or its subject is what constitutional texts define. Democracy means, on the contrary, that there is never *one* subject. Political subjects exist in the interval between different identities, in particular, between *man* and *citizen*. A process of political subjectivisation does not embed the power of man or that of the citizen but constructs a form of connection and disconnection between the two. In this process, man and citizen are used as political names, whose legal inscription is the product of a political process. They are also conflictual names, whose extension and comprehension are litigious, opening the space for their testing or verification. This is how they have been and can be used in democratic struggles. Citizenship means, on the one hand, the rule of equality among people who are inferior or superior as men, that is as private individuals subjected to the power of ownership and social domination. On the other, 'man' means the affirmation of the equal capacity of anyone, as opposed to the restrictions of citizenship, which exclude many categories of people from its scope or, place various problems out of the reach of the citizens. Man and citizen alternate in the role of the inclusive against the exclusive principle, of the universal against the particular. Democracy cannot be reduced to the universal power of the law against the particularity of interests, because the very logic of police means that the universal is continuously privatised. As a consequence, the universal must be continuously put into play and, for that to happen, it must be divided anew.

I tentatively made this point by commenting on the forms of feminist protest during the French Revolution.[9] Women had been denied the rights of citizens, according to the so-called republican principle that citizenship is the sphere of universality, while women's activity belongs to the particularity of domestic life. Women were in the sphere of the particular and, as a result, they could not be included in the universal. They had no will of their own and therefore they could not be political subjects. Against this 'self-evident' statement, Olympe de Gouges raised the well-known objection that since women were qualified to go to the scaffold, they were equally qualified to mount the platform of the Assembly. Her argumentation blurred the division of the spheres by setting up a universality entailed in the so-called particularity of bare life. Since women were sentenced to death as enemies of the Revolution, their bare life was political. On the scaffold, they were equal to men. The universality of the death sentence dismissed the 'self-evident' distinction between political and domestic life. They could therefore affirm their rights 'as citizens'. Their affirmation demonstrated that, despite Burke or Arendt, women did not have the rights that they had and had the rights that they did not have. On the one hand, they were deprived of the rights belonging to all 'free and equal' men, according to the Declaration of Rights, and demanded the rights denied to them. On the other, they demonstrated their political capacity, through their protest. They showed that since they could enact those rights, they actually possessed them.

A democratic process entails creating forms of subjectivisation in the interval between two identities; creating cases of universality by playing on the double relationship between the universal and the particular. Democracy cannot be predicated merely on the universality of the law, because that universality is ceaselessly privatised by the logic of governmental action. The universal must be supplemented by forms of subjectivisation and by cases of verification that resist the relentless privatisation of public life.

Privatisation takes two forms. Its explicit form denies political rights to parts of the population, on sexual, social or ethnic grounds. Its implicit form restricts the sphere of citizenship to a definite set of institutions, problems, agents and procedures. While the former looks outdated in the West, the latter, on the contrary, is a major contemporary problem. Over the last thirty years, the soft name of modernisation or the blunt name of the neo-conservative revolution have been used to reverse the democratic process, which had widened the public sphere by turning matters of 'private life', such as work, health and pensions, into public concerns related to equal citizenship. The stakes behind the reform of the 'social' or the 'welfare' state are much greater than the balance between public and private provision of services and utilities. The stake behind the regulation of work and health is the understanding of the 'common' of community. The line separating the political sphere of citizenship from the social sphere ruled by private arrangements determines who is able or not to participate in public affairs.

During the long strike by public transport workers in France in the winter of 1995, many Arendtian and Straussian arguments were heard contrasting private and financial interests to the political search for the common good and the ability to care for future generations. In the course of the strike, it became increasingly clear, however, that its main object was to decide whether a specific group of men and institutions had the exclusive power of determining the future of the community. The canonical distinction between the political and the social is in fact a distinction between those who are regarded as capable of taking care of common problems and the future and, those regarded unable to go beyond private and immediate concerns. The whole democratic process is about the displacement of this boundary.

I shall conclude by returning to my starting point. The question was, how to understand the paradox, which places democracy in opposition to itself. How to move from the oft-repeated statements about the uncertainty of the name and the contradictions of the actuality to a more radical interpretation of democratic self-difference. In *Spectres of Marx*, Derrida comments on Fukuyama's thesis about the historical achievement of liberal democracy, aiming to reopen the gap beneath the self-satisfied triumphalism of 'liberal democracy': 'It must be cried out, at a time when some have the audacity to neo-evangelize in the name of the ideal of a liberal democracy that has finally realized itself as the ideal of human history: never have violence, inequality, exclusion, famine, and thus economic oppression affected as many human beings in the history of the world and of humanity.'[10] To reopen the gap, Derrida opposed a *democracy to come* to a democracy which has reached itself or reached its *self*. A democracy to come will not arrive in the future but, it is a democracy emploted within a different time. The time of a 'democracy to come' is the time of a promise, which must be kept although – and because – it can never be fulfilled. It is a democracy which can never 'reach itself', catch up with itself, because it involves an infinite openness to that which comes – and to the infinite openness to the Other or the newcomer.

I cannot but agree with this principle. Derrida contrasts an other democracy to the so-called 'liberal democracy', placing two temporalities in the same time and two spaces in the same space. But there is a problem in the alleged opposition between the two democracies.

Derrida puts liberal democracy as a form of government on one side and places the infinite openness to the newcomer and the infinite expectation of the event, which evades all expectation, on the other. In my view, what disappears in this opposition between an institution and a transcendental horizon is democracy as practice. This practice leads to the political invention of the Other or the *heteron*; a process of political subjectivisation, which keeps creating 'newcomers', new subjects enacting the equal power of whoever and constructing new words about community in the given common world. To ignore the political power of *heterology* means to be trapped in a simple opposition: 'liberal democracy', on one side, which actually means oligarchy, embodying the law of the self and, a 'democracy to come', viewed as the time and space of an unconditional openness to the event and to otherness, on the other. This amounts to the dismissal of politics and to a form of substantialisation of otherness. The refusal of the allegedly democratic substantialisation of self leads symmetrically to the substantialisation of the Other, the sign of what can be called the contemporary ethical trend. Reference to the event and to the 'infinite respect for otherness', which are contrasted to democratic *autonomy*, are a commonplace in the current ethical trend. But these references may be interpreted differently and lead to very different conclusions.

Let us consider, for instance, the interpretation of the rights of the Other presented by Jean-François Lyotard at the Amnesty International lecture on human rights.[11] For Lyotard, the 'infinite respect for otherness' means obedience to the power of the Other – as the Freudian *Thing* or the Judaic Law – to which the human is a hostage or slave. The dream of the Enlightenment and of emancipation turns out to be the harmful will to deny the law of heteronomy, a will which could be seen as the cause of totalitarianism and of the Nazi genocide. As a consequence, the rights of the Other ultimately lead to the justification of the military campaigns against the axis of Evil. Ethics, otherness and the infinite respect for otherness become a kind of 'new Gospel', legitimising the practice and ideology of 'liberal democracy'.

Derrida is certainly far removed from such an interpretation of the Levinasian Other and from the ethical trend. In absolute contrast to Lyotard, he ties up the ethical injunction with a horizon of emancipation. He clearly contrasts the messianic promise and obedience to the Law. But in his attempt to avoid any pre-emptive identification of the event, the other or the infinite, he has to go through an endless process of deconstruction, crossing-out and *apophansis*. This ethical overstatement of otherness necessarily leads to a vacillation between two problematic interpretations. Either deconstruction asserts a radical law of heteronomy supporting ultimately the campaigns of the soldiers of God or, it insists on the infinite task of crossing out all pre-emptive identifications of the Other.

Derrida's conceptualisation gives both not enough and too much to democracy. Not enough, because democracy is more than the state practice of 'liberal democracy'. Too much, because democracy is less than the infinite openness to the Other. There is not *one* infinite openness to otherness but many ways of inscribing the part of the other. For my part, I tried to conceptualise democratic practice as the inscription of the part of those who have no part – which does not mean the 'excluded' but anybody or whoever. Such an inscription is made by subjects who are 'newcomers', who allow new objects to appear and become common concerns and new voices to appear and to be heard. In this sense, democracy is one of many ways of dealing with otherness. Its inventions of subjects and objects create a specific time, the broken time and intermittent legacy of emancipation. In my view, we must still think and act in this broken time instead of invoking a messianic time.

We should not ignore the reverse side of my position. Derrida speaks at a moment and for a time when the very nature of the 'break' is at stake and the following question arises. Can the figure of the *demos*, which has been staged so far within the nation-state, meet the demands of a cosmopolitan politics? While the 'disappearance' of the nation-state is debatable, one cannot deny that democracy today must come to terms with a cosmopolitan order. Derrida's answer is to call for a 'new International'. The forms of this new International are not clear. The main question is whether it should be conceptualised in political or 'ethical' terms. To do it politically, the 'infinite respect for the other' must take on the democratic contours of a multiplicity of forms of inscription of otherness, forms of alteration or dissensus instead of the infinite expectation of the Event or the Messiah.

Notes

1. Plato, *Menexenus*, 238c–238d.
2. J. Derrida, *Politics of Friendship* (London: Verso, 1997) 93–113 [The specific passage from *Menexenus* that Rancière refers to can also be found on p. 95 of Derrida's Book, N.E.].
3. M. Crozier, S. P. Huntington, J. Watanuki, *The Crisis of Democracy – Trilateral Commission Task Force Report no. 8* (New York: NYU Press, 1975).
4. J-C. Milner, *Les Penchants criminels de l'Europe démocratique* (Paris: Éditions Verdier, 2003).
5. B. Levy, *Le Meurtre du Pasteur* (Paris: Éditions Verdier, 2004).
6. Plato, *Republic*, book VIII, 563c–d.
7. Plato, *The Laws*, book III, 690c.
8. G. Agamben, *Homo Sacer* (Stanford: Stanford University Press, 1998).
9. Cf. J. Rancière, 'Who is the Subject of the Rights of Man', 103/2 *South Atlantic Quarterly*, Spring/Summer 2004.
10. J. Derrida, *Specters of Marx* (New York: Routledge, 1994) 85.
11. J-F. Lyotard, 'The Other's Rights', in S. Shute and S. Hurtey (eds) *On Human Rights* (New York: Basic Books, 1994).

7
Derrida: the Gift of the Future

Drucilla Cornell

Like many others I have been shocked, if not horrified, by some of the brutal reactions to Derrida's death from headlines such as 'Why I do not mourn Derrida' to long, winding attacks on why Derrida and deconstruction simply do not matter. What was, and remains, so frightening about the name of Derrida that triggered a specific kind of brutality directed at him even in death? Perhaps, it is precisely because Derrida dared to insist on a future, to insist, indeed, that there can always be a future despite efforts to shut it down in the name of a world historical closure as the advent of a certain market capitalism that cannot be challenged.

To remind us that Derrida is the thinker of the future *par excellence* will undoubtedly come as no surprise. From his writing on unconditional hospitality, to the *arrivant*, to the event, Derrida writes often of the future 'to come' which is the other already with us – inscribed in our heart, as he is in mine, as a debt that can never be repaid but must always evoke our thanks. And yet, this future 'to come,' in that it is always what is 'to come,' is never reducible to what is 'yet to come' (as if the yet could be given any form in advance of the event itself). To quote Derrida:

> It is perhaps necessary to free the value of the future from the value of 'horizon' that traditionally has been attached to it – horizon being, as the Greek word indicates, a limit from which I pre-comprehend the future. I wait for it. I pre-determine it. And thus, I annul it.[1]

101

And yet, this is not all Derrida tells us of his wager on the future.

If there is a future or, as he would have liked to put it, if there is such a thing, there must be some opening that calls to us in the form of an appeal. This appeal of the other demands that we respond now; indeed, the mark we leave on the world we share will be inseparable from those infinite appeals made to us and how we responded when we were called. As Derrida tells us:

> A simple phrase takes its meaning from a given context, and already makes its appeal to another one in which it will be understood; but, of course, to be understood it has to transform the context in which it is inscribed. As a result, this appeal, this promise of the future, will necessarily open up the production of a new context, wherever it may happen. The future *is not present*, but *there is* an opening onto it; and because *there is* a future, a context is always open. What we call opening of the context is another name for what is still to come.[2]

Here, Derrida is speaking of his own work as it went against the current and how it was thought by him to be an ethical response to this future and to the revision of context that this other future demanded. Again, to quote Derrida:

> It is a matter of looking for something that is not yet well received, but that waits to be received. And one may posses a kind of flair for that which, going against the current, is already in touch with the possible reception. So – if I may refer to my own case – in all likelihood, each time I have attempted to make a gesture that was, as you said, bizarre or untimely, it was because I had the impression that it was demanded, more or less silently, by other areas of the field, by other forces, that were still in the minority, that were there. So there is a sort of calculation in the incalculable here, and the untimeliness is a sort of timeliness in the making.[3]

When Ann Snitow and I decided, in the fall of 2002, to form a peace group, I spoke to Derrida at length about how the kind of group we wanted to form was one that would be faithful to the timeliness still in the making, a timeliness that seems so pressing because of the 'event' of 9/11. I put event in quotation marks to remind us of

Derrida's very careful analysis of why and how 9/11 could be considered a major event.[4] Tragically, Derrida points out that the death of thousands, tens of thousands, and even hundreds of thousand of people is not enough to make an event. Nor was 9/11 'unforeseeable', in his sense of the word event. Strangely enough it was foreseen even in Hollywood movies like *The Siege*, where Annette Benning portrays a bad Muslim who is coming to get us. Of course, I am echoing Mahmood Mamdani's title here *Good Muslim, Bad Muslim* and the fantasies about the Muslim religion that have so easily circulated in the US media and even worse in the US academy.[5]

What made 9/11 an event for Derrida was something scary indeed: the triggering of what he calls an auto-immunitary response, by which he means a quasi-suicidal process in which a person, a society, and a culture works to destroy its own protection.[6] For Derrida, there were three dangerous auto-immunitary responses – what he called the cold war in the head, the horizon of the worst, and the vicious cycle of repression unleashed by the thought that the even worse is yet to come. This fear of 'the even worse is yet to come' from an elusive 'them' is what Derrida foresaw as a true threat to the future. Even if the future remains 'yet to come' we can be shut away from it. By not exercising our responsibility, we can politically and ethically foreclose what is philosophically impossible to disavow.

Myself and Ann wanted to name this group faithfully, according to a different timeliness that we hoped to be part in making. Derrida insisted that we must somehow incorporate the word 'future' into the name of the group. Inspired by the words of the wonderful poet Alicia Ostriker and echoing the words of a certain feminist movement, we also knew that the group must be named with the words 'take back'. The inspiration of the two merged and the group was named 'Take Back the Future'. In all seriousness we saw in that name an urgent call to action. It was a call to action that must work to help revise the context in which we who live in New York City post 9/11 are surviving.

It is this sense of 'the future' I wish to emphasise in Derrida. It is something that can be taken away and something we are responsible for. As he reminds us, this call dictates a criticism of a 'religion of capital that institutes its dogmatism under new guises, which we must also learn to identify – for this is the future itself, and there will be none otherwise'.[7] For what is at stake in this criticism is the future itself and there will be no future without this. There is a deep, profound, and scary sense in which the future and our responsibility for the future cannot be in any other hands but our own.

It is up to us to take on the task of bringing into existence a timeliness still in the making, and if we do not take up such a task there is no alibi excusing our not doing so. Nor is there an alibi in often made accusations that the task set forth by Derrida is too big, too infinite, and therefore suggesting that there is nothing for us to do. The opposite is the case. Of course, I am writing of a specific, or *certain*, Derrida (to use one of his favourite words). To understand more deeply what is meant in the evocation of the word future, we must remember that Derrida had a complicated relationship to the imagination, perhaps one that is more complicated than he himself at times would allow. There is the Derrida who frequently echoes the Sartrean theme that the image is death, that our imagination intends nothingness. In this view, the imagination is both the cause of our 'nausea' and the basis of our freedom. But in his essay on Nelson Mandela, we see Derrida admiring Mandela for admiring the law and, indeed, for exemplifying it. Perhaps, this work is one of the most powerful examples of Derrida attempting to call forth from the future the possibility of justice today.

Here, Derrida is appealing to something close to the Kant of *The Critique of Judgment*.[8] In that work, Kant describes how the schematising power of the imagination can function to provide criteria of exemplary validity for moral judgement. Morality could not work effectively without the imagination's ability to narrate particular stories, which exemplify an otherwise abstract rule. In a sense, then, the moral law shows itself as an actual or particular person's response to it. Without this imaginative ability to evoke exemplary figures and narratives, and indeed by so doing to identify with their actions, it would be difficult to sustain the appeal to moral sentiment, as Mandela does in his famous trial to which Derrida refers. Mandela figures this admiration for the law not only by embodying this respect for the law in his life, but by portraying himself as one who respects the law by placing himself under it.

When we admire Mandela as an exemplar of the law we are also pulled toward the respect it demands of us. Derrida himself witnesses to his own identification with Mandela's admiration for the law by admiring that very admiration, and by so doing, he gets close to a Kantian exemplary imagination which works by this act of witnessing through intuition rather then mere abstraction. Derrida tells us:

> So he presents himself in this way. He presents himself in his people, before the law. Before a law he rejects, beyond any doubt, but which he rejects in the name of a superior law, the very one he declares to admire and before which he agrees to *appear*. In such a presentation of the self, he justifies himself in resuming his history, which he reflects in a single center, a single and a double center, his history and that of his people. Appearance: they appear together, he becomes himself again appearing before the law that he summons as much as he is summoned by it. But he does not present himself *in view* of a justification, which would follow his appearance. The presentation of the self is not *in the service* of the law, it is not a means. The unfolding of this history is a *justifica-tion*, it is possible and has meaning only before the law. He is only what he is, he, Nelson Mandela, he and his people, he has presence only in this movement of justice.[9]

Derrida calls us to identify with Mandela's identification of the moral law and with the command of justice as what constitutes who Mandela is. He does not only call us to identify with him, allowing his inscription of the law in his acts of admiration to reproduce a configuration of the moral doctrine within the context of the unjust system of apartheid, but he also tries to render visible the law to which the whites have blinded themselves. Again to quote Derrida:

> It tries to open up the eyes of the whites; it does not reproduce the visible, it produces it here. This reflection makes visible a law that in truth does more than reflect, because this law, in its phenome-non, was invisible – had become or continued to be invisible. Transporting the invisible into the visible, this reflection does not proceed from the visible, rather it passes through understanding. More exactly, it reveals to understanding what goes past under-standing and only relates to reason. It was a first reason, reason itself.[10]

We are reminded of Merleau Ponty's view, in which we see forms of being, including symbolic being, only as they appear from a perspective, leaving alongside what is visible a trace of the invisible.

The white nation had rendered a law that could not reflect on itself, because it denied what it claimed to embody: the law, the one nation of South Africa. By rejecting the law that inverts its own universality, Mandela reflects on the meaning of what this universality has promised but not delivered. Again, to quote Derrida:

> But, another inflection, if the testament is always made in front of witnesses, a witness in front of witnesses, it is also to open and enjoin, it is also to confide in others the responsibility of their future. To bear witness, to test, to attest, to contest, to present oneself before witnesses. For Mandela, it was not only to show himself, to give himself to be known, him and his people, it was also to reinstitute the law for the future, as if, finally, it had never taken place. As if, having never been respected, it were to remain, this arch-ancient thing that had never been present, as the future even – still now invisible.[11]

In this sense, Mandela, presenting and representing himself as the one who respects the law that has been rendered invisible in the legal system of apartheid, works to name the unnameable, at least under that system: the demands of blacks are not only the demands of human beings but their demand, and only their demand, can configure and bring into visibility the promise of universality. In a sense, then, Mandela's appeal to conscience is not only a memory but a promise to future witnesses who will, like him, exemplify and respect the law in their lives and the continuing struggle against apartheid. Simply put, Derrida says that the moral power of Mandela's testament to his own conscience evoking future witnesses who can hear his voice and receive his message proceeds through the exemplary or testimonial imagination. Truly, it can not do otherwise, for the law to which he subjects himself must be rendered visible if it is to be witnessed to. The exemplary imagination did not itself originate in Mandela, rather he simply answered its call and in so doing was comported toward a future possibility for a new South

Africa. However, Mandela is not alone in this calling, which is always reaching out to all of us, a calling that is perhaps one of our greatest inheritances of the future.

Derrida writes so beautifully of our obligation as heeding a 'timeliness in the making', which as he puts it is 'virtual, inhibited – it waits, pregnant with possible receivability'.[12] Derrida is to my mind so threatening to others because he adamantly and persistently heeded the forces that are silent, 'still in the minority but there'. He never did stop heeding those voices, as he was still signing petitions on the day he made his last journey to the hospital.

It is this injunction that 'we must act now' that is perhaps so forcefully felt at the moment of his death. For this now, this injunction that we must act immediately, is inseparable from Derrida's own thinking on death. As Derrida writes:

> Only a mortal can speak of the future in this sense, a god could never do so. So I know very well that all of this is a discourse – an experience, rather – that is made possible as a future by a certain imminence of death.[13]

The imminence here is that death may arrive at any moment. Heidegger discusses this brilliantly in *Being and Time* and the fact that death may arrive at any moment gives justice to the character of an immediate injunction. To be faithful to the future, then, is to open ourselves to the address, 'what are you doing today?'

Ultimately, it is this call to responsibility, seen as unavoidable and infinite, combined with the 'promise of the future that always might be' that made Derrida so terribly threatening to so many who would tell us that there is no future, and those who hold on to it with fidelity are nothing but fools and dreamers. In his 'adieu' to Emmanuel Levinas, Derrida writes that 'adieu' greets the other beyond being in what is signified, and here he quotes Levinas, 'beyond being by the word glory'. We may leave Derrida in his glory if we allow ourselves to accept the responsibility he entrusted us with. It is a responsibility toward the future that is always here 'to be received', and paradoxically in the best sense of the word 'to come'. My prayer for all of us, for myself, for my daughter, and to him is the gratefulness that lies in the hope he has left open in that entrustment.

Notes

1. J. Derrida, and M. Ferrari, *A Taste for the Secret*, trans. G. Donis (Cambridge: Polity, 2001) 20.
2. Ibid., pp. 19–20.
3. Ibid., p. 16.
4. See generally, G. Borradori, *Philosophy in a Time of Terror: Dialogues with Jürgen Habermas and Jacques Derrida* (Chicago: University of Chicago Press, 2003), Part 2.
5. See generally, M. Mandami, *Good Muslim, Bad Muslim: America, the Cold War, and the Roots of Terror* (New York: Pantheon, 2004).
6. See generally, G. Borradori, *Philosophy in a Time of Terror*, Part 2.
7. J. Derrida, *Other Heading: Reflections on Today's Europe*, trans. P-A Brault and M. Naas (Indianapolis: Indiana University Press, 1992) 77.
8. I. Kant, *The Critique of Judgment*, trans. J. C. Meredith (Oxford: Clarendon Press, 1978).
9. J. Derrida, 'The Laws of Reflection: Nelson Mandela, in Admiration', trans. M. A. Caws and I. Lorenz, in J. Derrida and M. Tlili (eds) *For Nelson Mandela* (New York: Henry Holt, 1987) 27.
10. Ibid., p. 23.
11. Ibid., p. 37.
12. Derrida, *A Taste for the Secret*, p. 16.
13. Ibid., p. 23.

8
A Plea for a Return to *Différance* (with a Minor *Pro Domo Sua*)

Slavoj Žižek

Here is what a well-known Slovene Catholic intellectual, ex-minister of culture and ex-ambassador of Slovenia to France, in short, an ethically corrupted nobody posing as a high Christian ethical authority, wrote apropos Derrida's untimely death without the letters written turning red out of shame:

> the only weapon is rebellion and destruction, as the recently deceased apostle Jacques Derrida taught us. Wherever you see a window, throw a brick into it. Where there is a building, there must be a mine. Where there is a high-rise building, a bin Laden should come. Where there is any kind of institution, law or link, one should find a falsification, a 'law' of the street or of the underground.[1]

Are lines like these not an indication of the rise of a new barbarism in today's intellectual life? Such phenomena are not limited to marginal countries like Slovenia. In the homeland of Empire, theories are emerging too which explain, for example, why the Frankfurt School appeared on the scene at a precise historical moment. When the failure of the socio-economic Marxist revolutions became apparent, the conclusion was drawn that the failure was due to an underestimation of the depth of western Christian spiritual foundations. As a result, the accent of subversive activity shifted from political and economic struggle towards a 'cultural revolution' and the patient intellectual-cultural work of undermining national pride, family, religion and spiritual commitments. The spirit of sacrifice for one's country was dismissed as involving the 'authoritarian personality'; marital fidelity was supposed to express pathological sexual repression; following Benjamin's thesis that every document of culture is also a document of barbarism, the highest achievements of western culture were denounced for concealing the practices of racism and genocide.

The main academic proponent of this new barbarism is Kevin MacDonald who, in his *The Culture of Critique*, argues that certain twentieth century intellectual movements led by Jews have changed European societies in fundamental ways and destroyed the confidence of western man. These movements were designed, consciously or unconsciously, to advance Jewish interests even though they were presented to non-Jews as universalistic and even utopian.[2] One of the most consistent ways in which Jews have advanced their own interests has been to promote pluralism and diversity – but only for others. Since the nineteenth century, Jews have led movements which tried to discredit the traditional foundations of gentile society such as patriotism, racial loyalty, the Christian foundation for morality, social homogeneity, and sexual restraint. MacDonald devotes many pages to *The Authoritarian Personality* (1950),[3] a collective project co-ordinated by Adorno, the purpose of which was, for MacDonald, to make every group affiliation sound as if it were a sign of mental disorder. Every noble sentiment, from patriotism to religion to family and race loyalty, was disqualified as a sign of a dangerous and defective 'authoritarian personality'. Because drawing distinctions between different groups is illegitimate, all group loyalties – even close family ties – were called 'prejudices'. MacDonald quotes approvingly Christopher Lasch's remark that *The Authoritarian Personality* leads to the conclusion that prejudice 'could be eradicated only by subjecting the American people to what amounted to collective psychotherapy – by treating them as inmates of an insane asylum'.[4] However, it is precisely the kind of group loyalty, respect for tradition and consciousness of differences central to Jewish identity that Horkheimer and Adorno described as mental illness in gentiles. According to MacDonald, these writers adopted what eventually became a favourite Soviet tactic against dissidents: anyone whose political views were different from theirs was insane. For these Jewish intellectuals, anti-Semitism was also a sign of mental illness: Christian self-denial and especially sexual repression caused hatred of

Jews. The Frankfurt school was enthusiastic about psychoanalysis, according to which 'Oedipal ambivalence toward the father and anal-sadistic relations in early childhood are the anti-Semite's irre-vocable inheritance.'[5] In addition to ridiculing patriotism and racial identity, the Frankfurt school glorified promiscuity and Bohemian poverty: 'Certainly many of the central attitudes of the largely suc-cessful 1960s counter-cultural revolution find expression in *The Authoritarian Personality*, including idealizing rebellion against parents, low-investment sexual relationships, and scorn for upward social mobility, social status, family pride, the Christian religion, and patriotism.'[6]

Although the 'French-Jewish deconstructionist Jacques Derrida' came later, he followed the same tradition when he wrote, 'the idea behind deconstruction is to deconstruct the workings of strong nation-states with powerful immigration policies, to deconstruct the rhetoric of nationalism, the politics of place, the metaphysics of native land and native tongue... The idea is to disarm the bombs... of identity that nation-states build to defend themselves against the stranger, against Jews and Arabs and immigrants.'[7] As MacDonald puts it, 'viewed at its most abstract level, a fundamental agenda is thus to influence the European-derived peoples of the United States to view concern about their own demographic and cultural eclipse as irrational and as an indication of psychopathology'.[8] This project has been successful: anyone opposed to the displacement of whites is routinely treated as a mentally unhinged 'hate-monger,' and when-ever whites defend their group interests they are described as psy-chologically inadequate – with, of course, the silent exception of the Jews themselves: 'the ideology that ethnocentrism was a form of psychopathology was promulgated by a group that over its long history had arguably been the most ethnocentric group among all the cultures of the world'.[9] We should have no illusions here: mea-sured by the standards of the great Enlightenment tradition, we are effectively dealing with something for which the best designation is the old orthodox Marxist term for 'bourgeois irrationalists': *the self-destruction of Reason*. The only thing to bear in mind is that this new barbarism is a strictly post-modern phenomenon, the obverse of the highly reflexive self-ironical attitude – no wonder that, reading authors like MacDonald, one often cannot decide if one is reading a satire or a 'serious' line of argumentation.

But the saddest surprise of all is to see some late representatives of the Frankfurt School, those theoretical descendants of those placed into the Jewish plot with Derrida by MacDonald, propose a kind of symmetrical reversal of the same story, which ends up in no less atrocious slander. Instead of being castigated as an agent of the Jewish plot, Derrida alongside Baudrillard and others is thrown into the 'postmodern' melting pot which, so the story goes, opens up the way for proto-Fascist irrationalism, if not directly providing the intellectual background for Holocaust denial. This brutal intolerance which masquerades as high moral concern, found its latest exponent in Richard Wolin whose *The Seduction of Unreason* is a worthy successor to Lukacs' most Stalinist work, the infamous *Die Zerstoerung der Vernunft* from the early 1950s. Wolin bombastically locates me, together with Baudrillard, among those who claimed that the US got what it deserved on 9/11:

> Traditionally, dystopian views of America have been the stock-in-trade of counterrevolutionary writers such as Maistre, Arthur de Gobineau, and Oswald Spengler. More recently, they have made inroads among champions of the postmodern left, such as Jean Baudrillard and Slavoj Žižek. In their theories, America represents the epitome of a postmodern, technological Moloch: a land devoid of history and tradition in which the seductions and illusions of a media-dominated mass culture have attained unchallenged hegemony. The postmodernists allege that the traditional orientations of family, community, and politics have ceded to the febrile delusions of 'hyperreality'. Today, we experience the reign of 'simulacra': media-generated copies, shorn of originals, that circulate autonomously. This attitude helps explain the enthusiasm with which Baudrillard greeted the September 11 attacks: a 'dream come true'.[10]

De Maistre, Gobineau, Spengler, Baudrillard, Žižek. Now I know where I belong: among the proto-Fascist irrationalists. The only consolation is that at least I find myself in good company, with people like Nietzsche and Adorno.[11] Wolin is at his lowest when he 'observes' what I wrote about the 9/11 events, as if I was describing just another mediatic spectacle, with no moral judgements implied. As 'proof', Wolin quotes a line from my 9/11 book: 'The unthinkable which happened was the object of fantasy, so that, in a way, America got what it fantasized about, and this was the greatest surprise',[12] claiming that the insertion of 'in a way' marks the ambiguity of my position. I carefully qualify my outrageous claim, without specifying what this qualification exactly means, so that I can have my cake and eat it. While making the claim that the United States got what it deserved, I also mark an empty distance to cover up the outrageous character of the claim. This line of argumentation is a simple empirical lie, if there ever was one. First, I do not claim that the United States got what they 'deserved', but what they 'fantasized' about, making it clear that when one gets one's fantasies, one ends up in a nightmare. Secondly, and much more importantly, I develop explicitly a little later, what I mean by this 'in a way' and reject Leftist *Shadenfreude*:

> The American patriotic narrative – the innocence under siege, the surge of patriotic pride – is, of course, vain; however, is the Leftist narrative (with its *Schadenfreude*: the US got what they deserved, what they were for decades doing to others) really any better? The predominant reaction of European, but also American, Leftists was nothing less than scandalous: all imaginable stupidities were said and written, up to the 'feminist' point that the WTC towers were two phallic symbols, waiting to be destroyed ('castrated'). Was there not something petty and miserable in the mathematics reminding one of the holocaust revisionism (what are the 6000 dead against millions in Ruanda, Kongo, etc.)? And what about the fact that CIA (co)created Taliban and Bin Laden, financing and helping them to fight the Soviets in Afghanistan? Why was this fact quoted as an argument *against* attacking them? Would it not be much more logical to claim that it is precisely their duty to get us rid of the monster they created? The moment one thinks in the terms of 'yes, the WTC collapse was a tragedy, but one should not fully solidarize with the victims, since this would mean supporting US imperialism,' the ethical catastrophe is already here: the only appropriate stance is the unconditional solidarity will *all* victims. The ethical stance proper is here replaced with the moralizing mathematics of guilt and horror, which misses the key point: the terrifying death of each individual is absolute and incomparable. In short, let us make a simple mental experiment:

if you detect in yourself any restraint to fully empathize with the victims of the WTC collapse, if you feel the urge to qualify your empathy with 'yes, but what about the millions who suffer in Africa...', you are not demonstrating your Third World sympathies, but merely the *mauvaise foi* which bears witness to your implicit patronizing racist attitude towards the Third World victims.[13]

Perhaps, after finding myself in the same boat with Derrida and others slandered by the moralising hypocrites, who effectively manipulate the memory of the 9/11 victims in order to score cheap 'theoretical' points, the time has come to draw the balance of my relations with Derrida, in a belated gesture of solidarity. Having written many pages in which I struggle with Derrida's work, now that the Derridean fashion is fading away, it is perhaps the moment to honour his memory by pointing out the proximity of my work with what Derrida called *différance*, this neologism whose very notoriety obfuscates its unheard-of materialist potential.

Derrida emphasised, in the last two decades of his life, how the more radical a deconstruction is, the more it has to rely on the inherent condition of deconstruction, the Messianic promise of justice. This promise is the true Derridean object of belief. Derrida's ultimate ethical axiom is that this belief is irreducible, 'undeconstructible'. Derrida can thus indulge in all kinds of paradoxes, claiming, amongst others, in his reflections on prayer, not only that atheists also pray, but that, today, it is perhaps only atheists who truly pray. By refusing to address God as a positive entity, they silently address the pure Messianic Otherness.[14]

It is here that one should emphasise the gap which separates Derrida from the Hegelian tradition:

> It would be too easy to show that, measured by the failure to establish liberal democracy, the gap between fact and ideal essence does not show up only in...so-called primitive forms of government, theocracy and military dictatorship...But this failure and this gap also characterize, *a priori* and by definition, *all* democracies, including the oldest and most stable of so-called Western democracies. At stake here is the very concept of democracy as concept of a promise that can only arise in such a

diastema (failure, inadequation, disjunction, disadjustment, being 'out of joint'). That is why we always propose to speak of a democracy *to come*, not of a *future* democracy in the future present, not even of a regulating idea, in the Kantian sense, or of a utopia – at least to the extent that their inaccessibility would still retain the temporal form of a *future present*, of a future modality of the *living present*.[15]

This is the difference between Hegel and Derrida at its purest. Derrida accepts Hegel's fundamental lesson that one cannot assert the innocent ideal against its distorted realisation. This holds not only for democracy, but also for religion; the gap which separates the ideal concept from its actualisation is already inherent in the concept itself. Derrida's claim is that in the same way that 'God already contradicts himself', all positive conceptual determination of the divine as a pure messianic promise already betrays it and that similarly one should also say that 'democracy already contradicts itself'. It is against this background that Derrida elaborates the mutual implication of religion and radical evil.[16] Radical evil (in political terms 'totalitarianism') emerges when religious faith or reason (or democracy itself) is posited in the mode of the future present. However, against Hegel, Derrida insists on an irreducible excess in the ideal concept which cannot be reduced to the dialectic between ideal and its actualisation. This is the messianic structure 'to come', the excess of an abyss which cannot ever be actualised in its determinate content.

Hegel's own position is here more intricate than may appear at first. His point is not that, through gradual dialectical progress, one can master the gap between concept and its actualisation and achieve the concept's full self-transparency ('absolute knowledge'). Rather, to put it in speculative terms, his point it to assert a 'pure' contradiction. This is not the contradiction between the undeconstructible pure Otherness and its failed actualisations or determinations but the thoroughly immanent 'contradiction', which precedes all Otherness. Actualisations and/or conceptual determinations are not 'traces of the undeconstructible divine Otherness', but just traces marking their in-between. To put it in yet another way, Derrida, in a kind of inverted phenomenological *epoche*, reduces Otherness to the 'to-come' of a pure potentiality and thoroughly de-ontologises it, bracketing its positive content. All that remains is the spectre of a promise;

and what if the next step is to drop this minimal spectre of Otherness itself, so that all that remains is the rupture, the gap as such which prevents entities to reach their self-identity? Recall the old reproach of the French Communist philosophers against Sartre's existentialism: Sartre jettisoned the entire content of the bourgeois subject, maintaining only its pure form; the next step is to throw away this form itself. One could claim *mutatis mutandis* that Derrida threw away all the positive ontological content of Messianism, retaining nothing but the pure form of its promise, and the next step is to throw away the form itself.

The same structure applies also to the passage from Judaism to Christianity. Judaism reduces the promise of the future life to a pure Otherness, to a messianic promise which will never become fully present and actualised (the Messiah is always 'to come'). Christianity, on the other hand, far from claiming the full realisation of the promise, accomplishes something far more uncanny. The Messiah is here, he has arrived, the final Event already took place, and yet the gap which sustained the messianic promise remains. One is almost tempted to propose a return to the earlier Derrida of *différance*: what if, as Ernesto Laclau among others has proposed,[17] Derrida's turn to the 'post-secular' messianism is not a necessary outcome of his initial 'deconstructionist' impetus? What if the idea of infinite messianic justice which operates in an indefinite suspension, always to come, as the undeconstructible horizon of deconstruction, already obfuscates the 'pure' *différance*, the pure gap which differentiates an entity from itself? Is it not possible to think this pure in-between prior to any notion of messianic justice? Derrida acts as if the choice is between a positive onto-ethics, the gesture of transcending the existing order towards another higher positive order, and the pure promise of spectral Otherness. What if we were to drop this reference to Otherness altogether?

Perhaps this brings us to the limits of the Derridean deconstruction of metaphysics. Three thinkers as different as Nietzsche, Heidegger and Derrida, all conceive their own age as that of the critical turning point of metaphysics. In their (our) time, metaphysics has exhausted its potentials, and the thinker's duty is to prepare the ground for a new, post-metaphysical, thinking. More generally, the entire Judeo-Christian history, up to our postmodernity, is determined by what one is tempted to call the Hölderlin paradigm which was first articulated in Augustine's *City of God*: 'Where the danger is grows also what can save us [*Wo aber Gefahr ist wächst das Rettende auch*]'. The present moment appears as the nadir in the long process of historical decadence (the flight of Gods, alienation, globalisation, etc.). But the danger of the catastrophic loss of the essential dimension of being-human also opens up the possibility of a reversal (*Kehre*): proletarian revolution, the arrival of new gods, which, according to the late Heidegger, can only save us, etc. Are we able to imagine a 'pagan' non-historical universe, a universe thoroughly outside this paradigm, a universe in which (the historical) time just flows, with no teleological curvature, in which the idea of a dangerous moment of decision (Benjamin's *Jetzt-Zeit*) out of which a 'bright future' which will redeem the past itself can emerge, is simply meaningless?

Although this Hölderlin paradigm is usually identified with Christianity, at its most radical, Christianity gives a unique twist to it. Everything that has to happen has already happened. There is nothing to wait for, we do not have to wait for the Event, the arrival of the Messiah. The Messiah has already arrived, the Event already took place, we live in its aftermath. This basic attitude of historical closure is also Hegel's message, and of his dictum that the Owl of Minerva takes off at dusk. It is difficult, but crucial, to grasp how this stance, far from condemning us to passive reflection, opens up the space for active intervention. The same applies for Kierkegaard who, in spite of his standard rumblings against the mass society of the 'present age', does not seem to rely on Hölderlin's paradigm of historicity and the *hubristic* self-perception of the thinker that such a view involves. There is nothing exceptional about our age; if anything, we live in ordinary and non-interesting times.

What is this *différance* that precedes the ethical commitment to the abyss of Otherness? On the southern side of the demilitarised zone in Korea, there is a unique visitor's site: a theatre building with a large screen-like window at the front, opening up onto the North. The spectacle people observe when they take seats and look through the window is reality itself or, rather, a kind of 'desert of the real': the barren demilitarised zone and beyond, a glimpse of North Korea. As if to comply with the fiction, North Korea has built in front of this theatre a pure fake, a model village with beautiful houses. In the evening, the house lights are switched on at the same time, although nobody lives in them. Is this not a pure case of the symbolic efficiency of the frame as such? A barren zone is given a fantasmatic status, elevated into a spectacle, solely by being enframed. Nothing substantially changes except that viewed through the frame, reality turns into its own appearance. An extreme case of such ontological comedy occurred in December 2001 in Buenos Aires, when Argentines took to the streets to protest against the current government, and especially against Cavallo, the Minister of Finance. When the crowd gathered around Cavallo's building, threatening to storm it, he escaped wearing a mask of himself, sold in novelty shops to people who wanted to mock him by wearing his mask. It seems that Cavallo at least learnt something from the widely spread Lacanian movement in Argentina, namely that a thing is its own best mask. What one encounters in tautology is pure difference, not the difference between one element and others, but the difference of the element from itself.

The fundamental lesson of Hegel is that the key ontological problem is not that of reality but of appearance. His key question is not 'are we condemned to the interminable play of appearances, or can we penetrate through their veil to the underlying true reality?' but 'how could in the middle of flat, stupid reality which is just there something like appearance emerges?' This minimal ontology is that of the Moebius band, of the curved space that is bent onto itself. All that is needed to intervene into the Real is an empty frame, so that the same things we saw before 'directly' are now seen through the frame. A certain surplus-effect is thus generated which cannot simply be cancelled through 'demystification'. It is not enough to display the mechanism behind the frame because the effect of staging within the frame acquires an autonomy of its own. How is this possible? Only one conclusion can account for this gap: there is no 'neutral' reality within which gaps occur and in which frames isolate domains of appearances. Every field of 'reality' (every 'world') is always-already enframed, seen through an invisible frame. However, the parallax of the two frames is not symmetrical, composed of two incompatible perspectives on the same x. There is an irreducible asymmetry between the two perspectives, a minimal reflexive twist. We do not have two perspectives, we have one perspective and what eludes it; the other perspective fills in the void of what we could not see from the first perspective.

One of the minimal definitions of a modernist painting concerns the function of its frame. The frame of the painting in front of us is not its true frame. There is another, invisible frame, the frame implied by the structure of the painting, the frame that enframes our perception of the painting. These two frames by definition never overlap – an invisible gap separates them. The pivotal content of the painting is not rendered in its visible part, but is located in this dislocation of the two frames, in the gap that separates them. This dimension in-between-the-two-frames is obvious in Kazimir Malevich; what is his *Black Square on White Surface* if not the minimal marking of the distance between the two frames? Again recall Edward Hopper's lone figures in office buildings or diners at night, where it seems as if the picture's frame has to be redoubled with another window frame; or, in the portraits of his wife who, close to an open window, is exposed to sun rays. Here we have the opposite excess of the painted content itself as regards what we effectively see, as if we see only the fragment of the whole picture, the shot with a missing counter-shot. Again, recall the droplets of sperm and the small foetus-like figure from *The Scream* squeezed between the two frames in Edvard Munch's *Madonna*. The frame is always-already redoubled: the frame within 'reality' is always linked to another frame enframing 'reality' itself.[18] Once introduced, the gap between reality and appearance is thus immediately complicated, reflected-unto-itself: once we get a glimpse, through the Frame, of the Other Dimension, reality itself turns into appearance. In other words, things do not simply appear, they appear to appear. This is why the negation of a negation does not bring us to a simple flat affirmation: once things (start to) appear, they not only appear as what they are not, creating an illusion; they can also appear to just appear, concealing the fact that they are what they appear.

It is this logic of the 'minimal difference', of the constitutive non-coincidence of a thing with itself, which provides the key to the central Hegelian category of 'concrete universality'. Let us take a 'mute' abstract universality, which encompasses a set of elements all of which somehow subvert, do not fit, this universal frame. In this case, the 'true' concrete universal is the distance itself, the universalised exception. And vice versa, the element which directly fits the universal is the true exception. Universality is not the neutral container of particular formations, their common measure, the passive (back)ground on which the particulars fight their battles, but the battle itself, the struggle leading from one particular formation to another. Recall Krzysztof Kieslowski's passage from documentary to fiction cinema. We do not simply have two species of cinema, documentary and fiction. Fiction emerges out of the inherent limitation of the documentary. Kieslowski's starting point was that of all cineasts in the Socialist countries, that is the conspicuous gap between the drab social reality and the optimistic, bright image pervading the heavily censored official media. The first reaction to the fact that social reality was 'unrepresented' in Poland, as Kieslowski put it, was the move towards a more adequate representation of the real life in all its drabness and ambiguity – in short, an authentic documentary approach: 'There was a necessity, a need – which was very exciting for us – to describe the world. The Communist world had described how it should be and not how it really was...If something hasn't been described, then it doesn't officially exist. So that if we start describing it, we bring it to life.'[19]

Suffice to mention *Hospital*, Kieslowski's documentary from 1976, in which the camera follows orthopaedic surgeons on a 32-hour shift. Instruments fall apart in their hands, the electrical current keeps breaking, there are shortages of the most basic materials, but the doctors persevere hour after hour, and with good humour. Eventually, however, the obverse experience sets in, best captured by the slogan used recently to publicise a Hollywood movie: 'It's so real, it must be a fiction!' At the most radical level, one can render the Real of subjective experience only in the guise of a fiction. Towards the end of the documentary *First Love* (1974), in which the camera follows a young unmarried couple during the girl's pregnancy, through their wedding and the delivery of the baby, the father is shown holding the newly born baby in his hands and crying. Kieslowski reacted to the obscenity of such unwarranted probing into the other's intimacy with the 'fright of real tears'. His decision to pass from documentaries to fiction films was thus, at its most radical, an ethical one:

> Not everything can be described. That's the documentary's great problem. It catches itself as if in its own trap...If I'm making a film about love, I can't go into a bedroom if real people are making love there...I noticed, when making documentaries, that

the closer I wanted to get to an individual, the more objects which interested me shut themselves off. That's probably why I changed to features. There's no problem there. I need a couple to make love in bed, that's fine. Of course, it might be difficult to find an actress who's willing to take off her bra, but then you just find one who is... I can even buy some glycerine, put some drops in her eyes and the actress will cry. I managed to photograph some real tears several times. It's something completely different. But now I've got glycerine. I'm frightened of real tears. In fact, I don't even know whether I've got the right to photograph them. At such times I feel like somebody who's found himself in a realm which is, in fact, out of bounds. That's the main reason why I escaped from documentaries.[20]

The crucial intermediary in this passage from documentary to fiction is *Camera Buff* (1979), the portrait of a man who, because of his passion for the camera, loses his wife, child and job; a feature film about a documentary filmmaker. A domain of fantasmatic intimacy exists which is marked by a 'No trespass!' sign and should be approached only through fiction, if one is to avoid pornographic obscenity. This is why the French Veronique in *The Double Life of Veronique* rejects the puppeteer. He wants to penetrate her too much, which is why, towards the film's end, after he tells her the story of her double life, deeply hurt she escapes to her father.[21] The 'concrete universality' is a name for this process through which fiction explodes from within documentary. This way, the emergence of fiction cinema resolves the inherent deadlock of documentary cinema. In philosophy, the point is not to conceive eternity as opposed to temporality, but eternity as it emerges from within our temporal experience or, in an even more radical way, to conceive time as a subspecies of eternity, as Schelling did, as the resolution of a deadlock of eternity.

This brings us to the heart of the concept of concrete universality, which is not merely the universal core that animates a series of its particular forms of appearance. It persists in the very irreducible tension, non-coincidence, between these different levels. Hegel is usually perceived as an 'essentialist historicist', positing the spiritual 'essence' of an epoch as a universal principle which expresses itself in a specific way in each domain of social life. The modern principle of subjectivity, for instance, expresses itself in religion as Protestantism, in ethics as the subject's moral autonomy, in politics as democratic equality, etc. This view misses what one is tempted to call the 'temporal parallax': in the complex dialectic of historical phenomena, we encounter events or processes which, although they actualise the same underlying 'principle' at different levels, they cannot occur at the same historical moment for that very reason.

Recall the old debate about the relationship between Protestantism, the Kantian philosophical revolution and the French political revolution. Rebecca Comay recently refuted the claim that Hegel's critique of the French Revolution can be reduced to a variation of the 'German' idea, according to which the Catholic French had to perform the violent 'real' political revolution because they had missed the historical moment of Reformation. In this view, the Reformation had already reconciled the spiritual Substance and the infinite subjectivity sought after by the revolutionaries in social reality. In this standard view, the German ethico-aesthetic attitude 'sublates' revolutionary violence in the inner ethical order, thus enabling the replacement of the abstract 'terrorist' revolutionary freedom by the concrete freedom of the State as an aesthetic organic Whole. However, the temporality of the relationship between the French political revolution and the German spiritual reformation is ambiguous. All three possible relations seem to overlap. First, the idea of 'sublation' points towards a succession. The French 'immediate' unity between the universal and the subject is followed by its sublation, the German ethico-aesthetic mediation. Secondly, we have the idea of a simultaneous choice (or lack thereof) which made the two nations follow different paths. The Germans opted for Reformation, while the French remained within the Catholic universe and had to take the tortuous route of violent revolution. However, the empirical fact that Kant's philosophical revolution preceded the French Revolution is not an insignificant accident. Kantian ethics encounters the ultimate consequence of its own 'abstract' character in the spectacle of revolutionary Terror, so that Kant's philosophy should be read retroactively, through the prism of the French Revolution which enables us to perceive its limitations:

> If [the Kantian moral view] presents itself as the narrative successor to the revolution, this is not because it logically fulfils or

supersedes it: Kant's critical venture *phenomenologically* succeeds the revolution that it *chronologically*, of course, anticipates only insofar as his text becomes legible only retroactively through the event that in institutionalizing the incessant short circuit of freedom and cruelty puts the project of modernity to its most extreme trial...the revolution itself inflicts on Kant's own text a kind of retroactive trauma.[22]

The revolutionary Terror is a kind of obscene double of Kant's ethical thought: its destructive violence merely 'externalises' the terrorist potential of Kant's thought. This is why it is hypocritical to reject the 'excesses' of the French Revolution from the standpoint of the 'German' moral view – and here resides Hegel's central insight. All its terrifying features found its counterpart in, are contained and *repeated* within, the Kantian spiritual edifice (and the term 'repetition' has to be given here the entire weight of Freud's *Wiederholungszwang*):

> The purity of the moral will can be no antidote to the terrifying purity of revolutionary virtue. All the logical problems of absolute freedom are essentially carried over into Hegel's analysis of Kantian morality: the obsessionality, the paranoia, the suspicion, the evaporation of objectivity, within the violent hyperbole of a subjectivity bent on reproducing itself within a world it must disavow.[23]

To the extent that we are dealing with a historical choice between the 'French' way of remaining within Catholicism and being obliged to engage in the self-destructive revolutionary Terror, and the 'German' way of Reformation, this choice involves the same elementary dialectical paradox as that between the two readings of 'the Spirit is a bone' also from *The Phenomenology of Spirit*. Hegel illustrates the latter through the phallic metaphor: the phallus as the organ of insemination as against the phallus as the organ of urination. Hegel's point is not that, in contrast to the vulgar empiricist mind which sees only urination, the proper speculative attitude has to choose insemination. The paradox is that the direct choice of insemination is the infallible way to miss it. It is not possible to choose directly the 'true meaning'; one has to begin by making the 'wrong' choice (of urination) and the true speculative meaning emerges only through the repeated reading, as the after-effect (or by-product) of the first, 'wrong', reading.

The same goes for social life in which the direct choice of the 'concrete universality' of a particular ethical life-world can only end in a regression to a pre-modern organic society that denies the infinite right of subjectivity as the fundamental feature of modernity. Since the subject-citizen of a modern state can no longer accept his immersion in some particular social role that confers on him a determinate place within the organic social whole, the only way to the rational totality of the modern State leads through revolutionary Terror. One should ruthlessly tear up the constraints of the pre-modern organic 'concrete universality', and fully assert the infinite right of subjectivity in its abstract negativity. In other words, the point of Hegel's analysis of revolutionary Terror is not the rather obvious insight into how the revolutionary project involved the unilateral direct assertion of abstract Universal Reason and was as such doomed to perish in self-destructive fury, because it was unable to organise the transfer of its revolutionary energy into a concrete stable and differentiated social order. Hegel's question was rather why, in spite of the fact that revolutionary Terror was a historical deadlock, we had to pass through it in order to arrive at the modern rational State. So, back to the choice between the Protestant 'inner revolution' and the French violent political revolution, this means that Hegel is far from endorsing the German self-complacent superiority ('we made the right choice and can thus avoid revolutionary madness'): precisely because Germans *made the right choice at the wrong time* – too early, in the age of Reformation – they cannot gain access to the rational State that would be at the level of true political modernity. One should take a step further. It is not only that the universal Essence articulates itself in the discord between its particular forms of appearance. This discord itself is propelled by a gap that pertains to the very core of the universal Essence. In his book on modernity, Fredric Jameson refers to the Hegelian 'concrete universality' in his concise critique of the recently fashionable theories of 'alternate modernities':

> How then can the ideologues of 'modernity' in its current sense manage to distinguish their product – the information revolution, and globalized, free-market modernity – from the

detestable older kind, without getting themselves involved in asking the kinds of serious political and economic, systemic questions that the concept of a postmodernity makes unavoidable? The answer is simple: you talk about 'alternate' or 'alternative' modernities. Everyone knows the formula by now: this means that there can be a modernity for everybody which is different from the standard or hegemonic Anglo-Saxon model. Whatever you dislike about the latter, including the subaltern position it leaves you in, can be effaced by the reassuring and 'cultural' notion that you can fashion your own modernity differently, so that there can be a Latin-American kind, or an Indian kind or an African kind, and so on...But this is to overlook the other fundamental meaning of modernity which is that of a worldwide capitalism itself.[24]

The significance of this critique reaches far beyond the case of modernity and addresses the fundamental limitation of nominalist historicising. The recourse to the concept of the 'multitude' ('there is not one modernity with a fixed essence, there are multiple modernities, each of them irreducible to others') is false not because it does not recognise a unique fixed 'essence' of modernity, but because multiplication functions as the disavowal of the antagonism that inheres to the notion of modernity as such. The falsity of multiplication resides in the fact that it frees the universal notion of modernity from its antagonism, of the way it is embedded in the capitalist system, by relegating capitalism to just one of its historical subspecies. One should not forget that the first half of the twentieth century already was marked by two big projects which perfectly fit this notion of 'alternate modernity': Fascism and Communism. Was not the basic idea of Fascism that of a modernity which provides an alternative to the standard Anglo-Saxon liberal-capitalism, of saving the core of capitalist modernity by casting away its 'contingent' Jewish-individualist-profiteering distortion? And was not the rapid industrialisation of the USSR in the late 1920s and 1930s also not an attempt at modernisation different from the western capitalist one? If we were to approach this inherent antagonism as the dimension of 'castration', and considering that according to Freud, the disavowal of castration is represented as the multiplication of the representatives of the phallus (a multitude of phalluses signals castration, the lack of the one), it is easy to conceive this multiplication of modernities as a form of fetishistic disavowal.

Frederick Jameson's critique of the notion of alternate modernities provides a model for the properly dialectical relationship between universal and particular: the difference is not on the side of particular content (as the traditional *differentia specifica*), but on the side of the universal. The universal is not the encompassing container of the particular content, the peaceful medium and background in the conflict of particularities. The universal 'as such' is the site of unbearable antagonism, self-contradiction and (a multitude of) its particular species are ultimately nothing but so many attempts to obfuscate/reconcile/master this antagonism. In other words, the universal names the site of a problem or deadlock, of a burning question; the particulars are the attempted but failed answers to this problem. The concept of State, for example, names the problem of how to contain the class antagonism in a society. All particular forms of State are so many (failed) attempts to propose a solution for this problem.

The same applied to the standard critique of Christian universalism. Its all-inclusive attitude (recall St Paul's famous 'There are no men or women, no Jews and Greeks') involves a thorough exclusion of those who do not accept the Christian communion. In other 'particularistic' religions (including Islam, despite its global expansionism), there is a place for others, who are tolerated, even if they are condescendingly looked upon. The Christian motto 'all men are brothers', however, means also that 'those who are not my brothers are not (even) men'. Christians pride themselves for overcoming the Jewish exclusivist notion of the chosen people and encompassing the entire humanity in God's plan. But there is a catch: in their very insistence that they are the chosen people with a privileged direct link to God, Jews accept the humanity of the other people with their false gods, while Christian universalism potentially excludes non-believers from the universality of the humankind.

But Christian universality is not an all-encompassing global medium where there is a place for all and everyone – it is rather the struggling universality, the site of a constant battle. Which battle, which division? To follow Paul, we can define this battle not as the division between Law and sin, but between, on the one side, the totality of Law with sin as its supplement and, on the other side, the way of Love. Christian universality is the universality which emerges at the symptomal point of those who are the 'part of no-part' of the global order. The reproach of exclusion gets it wrong because the Christian universality, far from excluding some subjects, is formulated from the position of those excluded, of those for whom there is no specific place within the existing order, although they belong to it. Universality is strictly co-dependent with this lack of specific place or determination.

To put it differently, the reproach to Paul's universalism misses the true site of universality: the universal dimension he opened up is not the 'neither Greeks nor Jews but all Christians', which implicitly excludes non-Christians. It is rather the difference between Christians and non-Christians which, as a difference, is universal, cutting across the entire social body, splitting, dividing from within every substantial identity. Greeks as well as Jews are divided into Christians and non-Christians. The standard reproach against Christianity is therefore misguided. The whole point of the Pauline notion of struggling universality is that true universality and partiality do not exclude each other, but that universal Truth is only accessible from a partial engaged subjective position.

For strategic reasons, my master-signifier for the 'minimal difference' is not *différance*, but *parallax*. The standard definition of parallax is the apparent displacement of an object (the shift of its position against a background), caused by a change in observational position that provides a new line of sight. The philosophical twist to be added is that the observed difference is not simply 'subjective', due to the fact that the same object which exists 'out there' is seen from two different stations, or points of view. It is rather that, as Hegel would have put it, subject and object are inherently 'mediated', so that an 'epistemological' shift in the subject's point of view always reflects an 'ontological' shift in the object itself. To put it in Lacanese, the subject's gaze is always-already inscribed into the perceived object itself, in the guise of its 'blind spot', of what 'in the object is more than the object itself', the point from which the object itself returns the gaze. 'Sure, the picture is in my eye, but me, I am also in the picture'.[25] The first part of this statement by Lacan designates subjectivisation, the dependence of reality on its subjective constitution, while the second provides a materialist supplement, re-inscribing the subject into its own image in the guise of a stain (the objectivised splinter in its eye). Materialism is not the direct assertion of my inclusion into the objective reality (such an assertion presupposes that my position of enunciation is that of an external observer who can grasp the whole of reality). It rather resides in the reflexive twist by means of which I myself am included into the picture constituted by me – it is this reflexive short-circuit, this necessary redoubling of myself as standing outside and inside my picture, that bears witness to my 'material existence'. Materialism means that the reality I see is never 'whole', not because a large part of it eludes me, but because it contains a stain, a blind spot, which signals my inclusion in it.

Nowhere is this structure clearer than in the case of Lacan's *objet petit a*, the object-cause of desire. The same object can all of a sudden be 'transubstantiated' into the object of my desire. What is to you just an ordinary object is for me the focus of my libidinal invest-ment, and this shift is caused by some unfathomable x, a *je ne sais quoi* in the object which cannot ever be pinned down to any of its particular properties. *Objet a* is therefore close to the Kantian tran-scendental object, since it stands for the unknown x, the noumenal core of the object beyond appearances, for what 'in you is more than yourself'. *L'objet petit a* can thus be defined as a pure parallax object. Not only its contours change with the shift of the subject; it only exists – its presence can only be discerned – when the landscape is viewed from a certain perspective. More precisely, the object *a* is the very cause of the parallax gap, that unfathomable x which forever eludes the symbolic grasp and thus causes the multiplicity of sym-bolic perspectives. This paradox is very precise: at the very moment when a pure difference emerges, a difference which is no longer a difference between two positively existing objects, but a minimal difference which divides one and the same object from itself, this difference 'as such' immediately coincides with an unfathomable object. In contrast to a mere difference between objects, the pure difference is itself an object. Another name for the parallax gap is therefore minimal difference, a 'pure' difference, which cannot be grounded in positive substantial properties. In Henry James' 'The Real Thing', the painter-narrator agrees to hire the impoverished 'true' aristocrats Major and Mrs Monarch as models for his illustra-tions of a *de luxe* book. However, although they are the 'real thing', their drawings appear a fake, so the painter has increasingly to rely on the vulgar couple of the cheap Cockney model Miss Churm and the lithe Italian Oronte, whose imitation of the high-class poses works much better. Is this not the unfathomable 'minimal difference' at its purest?

Jacques-Alain Miller recently proposed a Benjaminian distinction between 'constituted' and 'constituent' anxiety, a crucial distinction as regards the shift from desire to drive. While the former designates the standard notion of the terrifying and fascinating abyss of anxiety which haunts us with its infernal circle which threatens to draw us in, the latter stands for the 'pure' confrontation with the *objet petit a* as constituted in its very loss.[26] Miller is right to emphasise two features: the difference which separates constituted from constituent anxiety concerns the status of the object with regard to fantasy. In a case of constituted anxiety, the object dwells within the confines of a fantasy, while we only get the constituent anxiety when the subject 'traverses the fantasy' and confronts the void, the gap, filled up by the fantasmatic object. As Mallarmé put it in the famous bracketed last two lines of his 'Sonnet en-yx', the *objet a* is *'ce seul objet dont le Neant s'honore* [this sole object with which Nothing is honoured]'.

Miller's formula, while clear and convincing, misses the true paradox or, rather, ambiguity of the *objet a*. When he defines it as the object which overlaps with its loss or which emerges at the very moment of its loss (so that all its fantasmatic incarnations, from breasts to voice and gaze, are metonymic figurations of the void, of nothing), he remains within the horizon of desire – the true object-cause of desire is the void filled in by its fantasmatic incarnations. But as Lacan emphasises, the *objet a* is also the object of drive and the relationship here is thoroughly different. In both cases, the link between object and loss is crucial. But while in the case of *objet a* as the object-cause of *desire*, we have an object which is originally lost and coincides with its own loss, which emerges as lost, in the case of *objet a* as the object of drive, the 'object' is directly the loss itself. In the shift from desire to drive, we pass from the *lost object* to *loss itself as an object*. The weird movement called 'drive' is not driven by the 'impossible' quest for the lost object but is a push to directly enact the 'loss' – the gap, cut, distance – itself. A double distinction should be drawn. Not only between *objet a* in its fantasmatic and post-fantasmatic status, but also, within this post-fantasmatic domain itself, between the lost object-cause of desire and the object-loss of drive.

This is why one should not confuse the death drive with the so-called '*nirvana* principle', the trust towards destruction or self-obliteration. The Freudian death drive has nothing whatsoever to do with a craving for self-annihilation, for the return to the inorganic absence of any life-tension. It is, on the contrary, the very opposite of dying, a name for the 'undead' eternal life itself, for the horrible fate of being caught in the endless repetitive cycle of wandering around in guilt and pain. The paradox of the Freudian 'death drive' is therefore that it is Freud's name for its very opposite, for the way immortality appears within psychoanalysis, for an uncanny excess of life, an 'undead' urge which persist beyond the (biological) cycle of life and death, of generation and corruption. The ultimate lesson of psychoanalysis is that human life is never 'just life': humans are not simply alive, they are possessed by the strange drive to enjoy life in excess, passionately attached to a surplus which sticks out and derails the ordinary run of things.

It is wrong therefore to claim that the 'pure' death drive would have been the impossible 'total' will to (self)destruction, the ecstatic self-annihilation in which the subject would have rejoined the fullness of the maternal Thing, a will which is not realisable because it gets blocked, stuck to a 'partial object'. Such a notion re-translates death drive into the terms of desire and its lost object. It is in desire that the positive object is a metonymic stand-in for the void of the impossible Thing. It is in desire that the aspiration to fullness is transferred to partial objects – this is what Lacan called the metonymy of desire. One has to be precise, if we are not to miss Lacan's point (and thereby confuse desire and drive). Drive is not an infinite longing for the Thing which gets fixated onto a partial object – 'drive' is the fixation itself in which the 'death' dimension of every drive resides. Drive is not a universal thrust towards the incestuous Thing braked and broken up, it is rather the brake, a brake on instinct, its 'stuckness', as Eric Santner would have put it.[27] The elementary matrix of drive is not that of transcending all particular objects towards the void of the Thing (which is then accessible only in its metonymic stand-in), but that of our libido getting 'stuck' onto a particular object, condemned to circulate around it forever.

The basic paradox here is that the specifically human dimension – drive as opposed to instinct – emerges precisely when what was originally a mere by-product is elevated into an autonomous aim. Man is no longer 'reflexive' but, on the contrary, perceives as a direct goal what, for an animal, has no intrinsic value. In short, the zero-degree of 'humanisation' is not a further 'mediation' of animal activity or, its re-inscription as a subordinated moment of a higher totality (say, we eat and procreate in order to develop higher spiritual potentials), but the radical narrowing of focus, the elevation of a minor activity into an end-in-itself. We become 'humans' when we get caught into a closed, self-propelling loop of repeating the same gesture and finding satisfaction in it. We recall one of the archetypal scenes from cartoons: while dancing, the cat jumps up into the air and turns around its own axis but, instead of falling back down towards the earth's surface in accordance with the normal laws of gravity, it remains for some time suspended in the air, turning around in the levitated position as if caught in a loop of time, repeating the same circular movement. One also finds the same shot in some musical comedies which make use of the elements of slapstick. When a dancer turns around him- or herself in the air, s/he remains up there a little bit too long, as if, for a short period of time, s/he succeeded in suspending the law of gravity. And, effectively, is such an effect not the ultimate goal of the art of dancing? In such moments, the 'normal' run of things, the 'normal' process of being caught in the imbecilic inertia of material reality is for a brief moment suspended. We enter the magical domain of a suspended animation, of a kind of ethereal rotation which, as it were, sustains itself, hanging in the air like Baron Munchhausen who raised himself from the swamp by grabbing his own hair and pulling himself up. This rotary move-ment, in which the lineal progress of time is suspended in a repeti-tive loop, is drive at its most elementary. This, again, is 'humanisation' at its zero-level: this self-propelling loop which suspends/disrupts linear temporal enchainment.

The concept of drive makes the alternative 'either burned by the Thing or maintaining a distance' false: in a drive, the 'thing itself' is a circulation around the void (or, rather, hole, not void). To put it even more pointedly, the object of drive is not related to the Thing as a filler of its void. Drive is literally a counter-movement to desire, it does not strive towards impossible fullness and, being forced to renounce it, gets stuck onto a partial object as its remainder. Drive is quite literally *the very 'drive' to break the All of continuity in which we are embedded*, to introduce a radical imbalance into it, and the difference between drive and desire it precisely that in desire, this cut, this fixation onto a partial object, is 'transcendentalised', as it were, transposed into a stand-in for the void of the Thing.

This is also how one should read Lacan's thesis on the 'satisfaction of drives'. A drive does not bring satisfaction because its object is a stand-in for the Thing, but because a drive turns failure into a triumph as it were – in it, the very failure to reach its goal, the repetition of this failure, the endless circulation around the object, generates a satisfaction of its own. As Lacan put it, the true aim of a drive is not to reach its goal, but to circulate endlessly around it. In the well-known vulgar joke about a fool having his first intercourse, the girl has to tell him exactly what to do: 'See this hole between my legs? Put it in here. Now push it deep. Now pull it out. Push it in, pull it out, push it in, pull it out...' 'Now wait a minute', the fool interrupts her, 'make up your mind! In or out?' What the fool misses is precisely the structure of a drive which gets its satisfaction from the indecision itself, from repeated oscillation. In other words, what the fool misses is Derrida's *différance*.

Notes

1. A. Capuder, 'Vino in most', *Demokracija*, No. 50, year IX, Ljubljana, 9 December 2004, p. 9 (translation mine). Incidentally, does this 'where there is a high-rise building, a bin Laden should come' not sound as a new politicised version of Freud's *wo es war soll ich werden*? S. Freud, 'New Introductory Lectures on Psychoanlalysis', in J. Strachey et al. trans., *The Standard Edition of the Complete Psychological Works* (London: Hogarth Press, 1953–1974), Vol. XXII, p. 80.
2. K. B. MacDonald, *The Culture of Critique: an Evolutionary Analysis of Jewish Involvement in Twentieth-Century Intellectual and Political Movements* (Westport: Praeger, 1998).
3. K. B. MacDonald, *The Authoritarian Personality* (New York: Norton, 1982).
4. Ibid., p. 169.
5. Ibid., p. 145.
6. Ibid., p. 194.
7. Ibid., p. 201.
8. Ibid., p. 195.
9. Ibid., p. 232.
10. See R. Wolin, *The Seduction of Unreason: the Intellectual Romance with Fascism from Nietzsche to Postmodernism* (Princeton: Princeton UP, 2004),

23. See Georg Lukacs, *Die Zerstörung der Vernunft* (Berlin, 1953), trans. P. Palmer under the title *The Destruction of Reason* (London: Merlin, 1980).

11. The same line of attack was brought to an extreme by Jörg Lau in Germany, who, after the weird claim that I celebrate the 9/11 attack as the proper Lacanian political act, as the intervention in the Real which breaks the spell of capitalist ideological hallucinations, ends up indirectly characterising me as a pathological person – there is, in me, 'etwas Verkommenes, geistig Verwahrlostes' (Jörg Lau, 'Auf der Suche nach dem guten Terror: Über Slavoj Žižek', in *Merkur* 2/2003, 158–63). Is it necessary to add that I was not able to answer these defamations in *any* German printed medium?

12. Wolin, *The Seduction of Unreason*, p. 307.

13. Slavoj Žižek, *Welcome To the Desert Of the Real* (London: Verso Books, 2002) 86.

14. See J. Derrida, *Acts of Religion* (New York: Routledge, 2002).

15. J. Derrida, *Specters of Marx* (London: Routledge, 1994) 64–5.

16. See Jacques Derrida, 'Faith and Knowledge', in J. Derrida and G. Vattimo (eds) *Religion* (Stanford: Stanford University Press, 1998).

17. See Ernesto Laclau, *Emancipation(s)* (London: Verso Books, 1995).

18. Derrida, of course, developed this motif in great detail in his *La verité dans la peinture*, (Paris: Flammarion, 1988) [trans. G. Bennington and I. McLeod, *The Truth in Painting* (Chicago: University of Chicago Press, 1987)].

19. *Kieslowski on Kieslowski*, D. Stok (ed.) (London: Faber and Faber, 1993), 54–5.

20. Ibid., p. 86.

21. For a more detailed account of this passage, see Chapter 1 of S. Žižek, *The Fright of Real Tears* (London: BFI, 2001).

22. R. Comay, 'Dead Right: Hegel and the Terror', 103:2/3 *South Atlantic Quarterly*, Spring/Summer 2004, 393.

23. Ibid., p. 392.

24. F. Jameson, *A Singular Modernity* (London: Verso Books, 2002) 12.

25. J. Lacan, *The Four Fundamental Concepts of Psycho-Analysis* (New York: Norton, 1979) 63.

26. See J-A. Miller, 'Le nom-du-père, s'en passer, s'en servir', available on www.lacan.com.

27. See E. Santner, *On the Psychotheology of Everyday Life* (Chicago: University of Chicago Press, 2001).

9
The Late Derrida
J. Hillis Miller

Derrida is always late, *en retard*, the late Derrida. This is not because he was habitually late for appointments, lunch engagements or seminars. Far from it. He was even compulsively ahead of time, always a few minutes early. Nevertheless, Derrida was always late, always behind time, until the end. A good thing too. I promise sooner or later to show why.

'I could never tell a story'

Derrida more than once said that he could never tell a story. I suppose he meant that something in him resisted organising things neatly in a narrative, with a beginning, middle and end, such as Aristotle said all good plots (*muthoi*) should have. Derrida's *La Carte postale*,[1] however, can be seen as a novel, even, by certain definitions, as a brilliantly innovative 'postmodern' or at least 'modernist' novel. It tells, or appears to tell, with exorbitant obliqueness, a love story. A resistance to telling a story in straightforward chronological order is, however, a feature of twentieth-century western fiction from Conrad and Faulkner on. This resistance crosses the boundaries from modernist to postmodernist, and of course it is present in earlier fictions too. It is even present already in Cervantes, for example in 'The Dogs' Colloquy', one of the *Exemplary Stories*.[2] It is also one primary organising (or disorganising) feature of Sterne's *Tristram Shandy*,[3] along with its concomitant, digression.

In his last seminar series (2002–3), the second set on 'The Beast and the Sovereign', Derrida does once again tell a story. It is the story of me running towards death as death runs towards me. It is a story apropos of another famous story, Robinson Crusoe's response when he encounters the print of a naked foot in the sand. Derrida's improvisation on this episode, and on what Defoe tells the reader went on in Crusoe's mind after he saw the footprint, is wild and exuberant in a way characteristic of 'the late Derrida'. What Derrida writes is a story about a story about a story, three stories nested within one another. Derrida's discourse digresses suddenly from his improvisations on Crusoe's fear of that footprint to tell another story, this one inspired by a passage from John Donne that, says Derrida, suddenly comes into his mind apropos of Crusoe's fear of that naked footprint. In addition, no one can doubt, Derrida is obliquely telling his own story, expressing his own fear of death. He is even, in later seminars in the series, making a frightening story of his fear of being buried alive or eaten alive, apropos of a few phrases in *Robinson Crusoe*. The whole sequence in the novel from Crusoe's discovery of 'the Print of a Man's naked Foot on the Shore',[4] to Crusoe's actual encounter with Friday takes a good many pages. Derrida is especially interested, however, in Crusoe's initial reaction of abject terror and, within that, in the moment when Crusoe imagines that the footprint he has seen may be his own, so that he may be chasing and being chased by himself:

> In the middle of these Cogitations, Apprehensions and Reflections, it came into my Thought one Day, that all this might be a meer Chimera of my own; and that this Foot might be the Print of my own Foot, when I came on Shore from my Boat. This chear'd me up a little too, and I began to persuade my self it was all a Delusion; that it was nothing else but my own Foot, and why might not I come that way from the Boat, as well as going that way to the Boat, again, I consider'd also that I could by no Means tell for certain where I had trod, and where I had not; and that if at last this was only the Print of my own Foot, I had play'd the Part of those Fools, who strive to make stories of Spectres, and Apparitions; and then are frighted at them more than any body.[5]

Ghost stories, Defoe here says, raise the fearful ghosts they appear only to describe. Here is a part of the improvisation that Derrida develops, in ornate arabesque, on the theme that Defoe has established of the possibility that Crusoe has seen his own footprint and is frightened by the trace of his own uncanny double or *revenant*. Derrida makes quite a story of it, placing himself, as a good story-teller or narrator does, within the mind and feelings of his pro-tagonist. Derrida speaks eloquently for that imaginary terrorised subjectivity, first in free indirect discourse and then in the intimacy of an interior monologue. A fairly lengthy extract must be cited, since the word play, exuberant hyperbole, and constantly self-topping inventiveness, like a great Charlie Parker riff or a Bach fugue, are fundamental features of what is going on here in Derrida's language. I shall return later to the jazz/Bach analogy and its implications:

> *Enfin*, alors qu'il vient de poser sa Bible et de se réconforter par la prière, voilà qu'il se demande où il est, en quel lieu, quel aura été son chemin. Il se demande avec encore plus d'anxiété si cette empreinte de pied nu n'est pas celle de son propre pied? De son propre pied sur un chemin qu'il aurait déjà parcouru. Au fond, il n'arrive pas à décider si cette trace est ou non la sienne, une trace laissée sur un chemin dont il ne sait pas trop s'il l'a déjà foulé, frayé ou passé – ou non. Il n'en sait trop rien. Est-ce moi? Est-ce ma trace? Est-ce mon chemin? Est-ce le spectre de mon empreinte, l'empreinte de mon spectre? Suis-je en train de revenir? Suis-je ou ne suis-je pas revenant? Un revenant de moi-même que je croise sur mon chemin comme la trace de l'autre, sur un chemin qui est déjà un chemin de retour et de revenance, etc.? J'en sais trop rien, ou je n'en sais trop rien de la possibilité de ce double *uncanny, unheimlich*...
>   Il se fait peur. Il devient la peur qu'il est et qu'il se fait. Et toutes ces pages, parmi les plus extraordinaires du livre, celles qui le montrent, où il se montre en train de méditer, dans la terreur, sur cette trace de pied nu, ces pages devraient être lues pas à pas, et par exemple en parallèle avec la *Gradiva* de Freud, avec tous les *fantasmata*, à savoir les fantasmes et les fantômes qui reviennent sur l'empreinte d'un pas, ou d'un pied nu, *the print of a naked Foot*.[6]

[Finally, now that he has put down his Bible and has comforted himself with prayer, now he asks himself where he is, in what place and what his path has been. He asks himself with even more anxiety if that print of a naked foot is not that of his own foot? Of his own foot on a path he has already traversed. At bottom, he never comes to decide if that trace is or is not his own, a trace left on a path about which he doesn't really know whether he has already marked it out or passed there or not. He doesn't know anything at all about it, he knows that he knows nothing about it. Is it I? [*Est-ce moi?*] Is it my track? Is it the specter of my print, the print of my specter? Am I in the process of returning? Am I or am I not a ghost, a *revenant*? A *revenant* of myself which I cross on my path as the trace of the other, on a path which is already a path of return and of coming back, etc.? I don't know anything at all about it, or I know too well that I know nothing at all (*J'en sais trop rien, ou je n'en sais trop rien*) about the possibility of this uncanny, *unheimlich* double.

He makes himself afraid. He becomes the fear that he is and that he causes himself to have. And all these pages, among the most extraordinary in the book, those which show him, where he shows himself in the process of meditating, in terror, about the trace of a naked foot, these pages should be read step by step [*pas à pas*], and for example in parallel with Freud's *Gradiva*, with all the *fantasmata*, that is to say the phantasms and the phantoms who return on the imprint of a step, or of a naked foot, *the print of a naked foot*. (J. Hillis Miller translation)]

The reader will see how far Derrida goes beyond Defoe's words, while still responding responsibly to them. Defoe's ascriptions of fear to Crusoe are the product of a rationalist and empiricist early eighteenth-century, to which has been added a peculiar Defoesque form of slightly ironic English Protestant sensibility, along with a superstitious streak, that, as he says in one place, means he is not sure whether or not he believes in ghosts. I say ironic Protestant sensibility because Defoe is not Crusoe. Though only Crusoe speaks in *Robinson Crusoe*, nevertheless, a slightly amused and condescending Defoe may be glimpsed behind the terror Defoe ascribes to Crusoe at the 'meer' sight of a footprint in the sand. Derrida's words about Defoe's words, however, could only have been written by Derrida, and only by a Derrida concerned to make a certain reading of Heidegger as well as to appropriate *Robinson Crusoe* for his own ends. One might almost dare to say that Derrida turns *Robinson Crusoe* into a postmodern narrative, though just what that might mean is not all that easy to specify.

Derrida's Crusoe is imagined to ask himself where he is, in what place, and by what pathway he got there, as though he were just waking from sleep or suddenly waking into existence, like those Cartesian and post-Cartesian wakers that so fascinated Georges Poulet in *études sur le temps humain*.[7] For Crusoe to ask about his pathway or *chemin* is, like Descartes again, or like Heidegger after him, in Derrida's reading, to seek a method, a way forward. *Method* comes, etymologically, from Greek *meta* (after) plus *hodos* (road or journey). A good method follows after a track implicitly already laid out as a sure way to get where you want to go, a goal that is already there, waiting for you to get there. Derrida's Crusoe, however, is not so much anxious about the way forward, or even about the way he has got where he finds himself, as he is anxious about the question of whether he has been there before. It could be that he has no more than inadvertently retraced his steps. He has, it may be, travelled in a circle without intending it. He may have come back to meet up with his own footprint on the sand. To have done that would be uncanny, *unheimlich*. It would have that particular form of uncanniness Freud associated with encountering one's own ghostly double. Shelley's Zoroaster, to give one example, 'met his own image walking in the garden'.[8] To meet oneself would be even more terrorising than meeting the ghost of another. 'We have met the enemy, and he is us,' says Walt Kelly's Pogo.[9]

Revenant: the word means something that has come back, the return, it may be, of a repressed or forgotten trauma. It might be better, for my mental health, that I should successfully repress or forget such a trauma. Toni Morrison's *Beloved*[10] suggests that this might be the case with the facts of United States slavery. If Crusoe has travelled this path before, it was, Derrida says, without knowing it. This is expressed in a characteristic Derridean wordplay. Crusoe may have been 'describing' a trajectory without knowing it. But to describe, says Derrida, is also 'parcourir', to run through. To describe a journey is to make that journey. Crusoe does not know whether or not he decided to take this path once before and so is now haunted, so to speak by himself, or is himself now haunting his other self. He cannot decide whether this is his own footprint or not. Derrida stresses this absolute non-knowledge and this absolute inability to decide, whereas in *Robinson Crusoe*, Crusoe comes back some time later and discovers by careful measurement that a foot much bigger than his own made the footprint. It cannot be his own footprint.

Derrida's Crusoe expresses, on the contrary, a hyperbolic non-knowledge, just at the moment when he shifts from the third person to the first person, in a more or less untranslatable French idiom: *'J'en sais trop rien'*, or *'Je n'en sais trop rien'*, one of which means, literally, 'I know too much nothing of it', the other 'I don't know too much nothing of it'. Either locution could be translated, I suppose, as 'I know nothing whatsoever about it', or 'I know too well that I know nothing about it'. 'Is it me? Is it my trace? Is it my track? Is it the specter or my footprint, the imprint of my specter . . . Am I or am I not a revenant? . . . I know nothing at all about it . . . Who has decided what? and to go where?' and so on, in an amazing inexhaustible circling repetition of the same words or almost the same words.

I have compared this repetition with variations to Bach or jazz. Such repetition is an essential feature of the late Derrida style. Here the stylistic repetition mimes the experience of being haunted by oneself, of retracing a path already traversed and coming back incessantly to confront oneself either as the haunter or the haunted, or, rather, as both.

This doubling of the solitary self within itself empties out the self, or overfills it, so it is no longer unified, fixed and self-contained. This destruction of the unitary self is the goal towards which the whole passage moves. I am alone, completely alone. At the same time, I am accompanied by the other me, the other in me. My specular phantom or uncanny double puts me in the situation of not knowing whether I am myself or whether, if I look into the mirror, I shall see my own image there, or some stranger: 'the other man as me, me as another, I who am another'. (An echo of Arthur Rimbaud's *'Je est un autre.'*)[11] *J'en sait trop rien.* I know damn all about it.

The result is abject terror. This terror is generated by nothing more than seeing 'the print of a naked Foot' on the shore. Derrida makes the circular island, with its path around the perimeter, a figure for Crusoe's self-duplicating solitude. At the climax of this sequence, Derrida identifies *fear* as the chief feature of Crusoe's reaction to seeing the naked footprint. It is both generalised terror, the worst kind, and at the same time fear of himself. He becomes the fear that he is and that he has made himself into: '*Il se fait peur. Il devient la peur qu'il est et qu'il se fait.*'

What Derrida says has drifted pretty far away from Defoe's words, into a marvellous descant on their implications. He ends, however, with an exhortation to read again the words Defoe wrote, 'step by step', but in parallel with a reading of Freud's *Gradiva* essay ('Delusions and Dreams in Jensen's *Gradiva*').[12] To do that would be yet another digression or deviation from the straight path. But perhaps the proper methodological way can here proceed only by such sideways juxtapositions or detours.

The reader will note that Derrida's reading of *Robinson Crusoe* has one important peculiarity. This feature distinguishes what Derrida says from most recent scholarship. He focuses primarily on Crusoe's solitary experiences, his relations, one might say, to himself, whereas much current scholarship of the 'cultural studies' sort has been more concerned with Crusoe's enslavement of Friday, or with his ownership of slaves on his plantation in Brazil, or with his imperial sovereignty over his island as an example of European racist colonisation, or with Crusoe's role as an exemplary Protestant capitalist and *homo economicus*. All that is relatively less interesting to Derrida than Crusoe's exemplification of the solitude of Dasein in the world. 'Solitude (*Einsamkeit*)' is, after all, one of the fundamental themes of Heidegger's *Die Grundbegriffe der Metaphysik*,[13] the work that Derrida reads in tandem with *Crusoe*. Derrida weaves or wanders back and forth from one path to the other, from Heidegger to Defoe and back again, throughout the whole set of ten seminars.

What, exactly, motivates Derrida's repetitive style in these late seminars? Is it no more than a way of filling up enough pages to make a two-hour seminar? Or is it a pedagogical device, saying everything over a number of times to make sure that his auditors 'get it'? Or is it a product of Derrida's inexhaustible, fantastic, linguistic inventiveness? He can always think of a thousand different ways to say almost the same thing. Or, is at an attempt, by varying the phrasing, to get it right at last, to utter the Open Sesame that will lead to a direct confrontation with the 'wholly other'? Or is there some even deeper motivation? The pages that follow those I have cited from the second seminar may give a clue. After all he has said about Crusoe's fear that it may be his own footprint, Derrida is not yet finished. He draws breath, and, perhaps inspired by Defoe, perhaps inspired by his own train of thought generated by Defoe's words that he cites, in response to them, he suddenly remembers two lines from a poem by John Donne. They come from who knows where into his mind. That sets him off again on another extraordinary circular improvisation.

Running towards death, while death runs towards me

The improvisation is inspired (in the etymological sense of 'breathed in') by his reading aloud of the lines by Defoe I began by quoting. In Derrida's seminar, the citation comes after the commentary, preposterously, one might say, or metaleptically, the cart before the horse, whereas I have quoted it first. Citing Defoe leads Derrida to remember that Crusoe's fear leads him to retreat into his 'castle' and immure himself there in abject terror. Derrida's Crusoe feels, as we have seen, as if he were being pursued by himself as revenant, but that other self is really death. Time reverses, in a brilliantly succinct formulation in which the death towards which Crusoe runs, towards the future, is really running after him, from the past, or from the future anterior. It is as if he were already dead and as if everything that happens to him were happening not for the first time, but as repetition, as *revenance*. Tomorrow is really yesterday, in a perpetual *déjà vu*. The future is something already past. Perhaps. He really does not know anything at all about it. It is not something open to cognition:

> Il se sent suivi par une trace, en somme, chassé ou traqué par une trace. Voire par sa propre trace. Peut-être persécuté par lui-même et par sa propre revenance. Comme s'il vivait tout au passé de son propre passé comme avenir terrifiant. Il croit qu'il va bientôt mourir, qu'il court après sa mort ou que la mort lui court après, que la vie aura été si courte, et donc, comme s'il était déjà mort, à cause de cette course de vitesse avec sa revenance, tout ce qui lui arrive lui arrive non comme nouveau, neuf ou à venir mais comme (peut-être, il n'en sait trop rien) déjà passé, déjà vu, à venir comme hier et non comme demain.[14]

[He feels himself followed by a trace [*une trace*], in short, chased or tracked by a trace. That is to say, by his own trace. Perhaps persecuted by himself and by his own return. As if he lived entirely in the past of his own passing as a terrifying future. He believes that he is about to die, that he runs after his death, that life will have been so short, and therefore, as if he were already dead, because of this speed race with his ghostly return [*sa reve-nance*], everything that happens to him happens not as novel, new or to come, but as (perhaps; he doesn't know anything at all about it) already past, already seen [*déjà vu*], to come as yesterday and not as tomorrow. (J. Hillis Miller, translation)]

This frightening reflection reminds Derrida suddenly of two verses by Donne that just pop into his mind. The quotation: '*revient de je ne sais plus où à ma mémoire (tableau)* [comes from I don't know where into my memory (blackboard [*tableau*]).' I thought at first that this was a reference to Hamlet's phrase about 'the tablets of my memory', but then I saw that it must be a note to himself to write the lines on the blackboard (*tableau*) for his auditors to see, to have before their eyes as he goes on talking:

> I run to Death and Death meets me as fast
> And all my Pleasures are like Yesterday[15]

The passage from Derrida I cited a moment ago anticipates the essential points of what Derrida gets out of the two lines from Donne. That does not keep him, however, from writing an amazing commentary that goes on for six extraordinary pages more, too many to quote *in toto* here. I can only hope that all ten of these latest seminars will soon be published or made available online or in a Derrida archive. They are a work of great genius, comparable, in their strange combination of repetitive abstraction and a kind of eerie ethereal passion, to Wallace Stevens's late poems or to Beethoven's late quartets. Here, as a sample, is just the first two paragraphs of the improvisation on the two lines from Donne. The passage repeats over and over, like a dominant note in a musical development, the word 'hier', yesterday. Hier, hier, hier; yesterday, yesterday, yesterday, until the word almost loses all meaning and becomes a mere sound:

> Je cours vers la mort, je me précipite vers la mort et la mort vient à ma rencontre tout aussi vite. (Je cours sus à la mort, je cours à

mort (*I run to Death*) et mort me vient dessus, mort de rencontre me saisit, m'attrape ou me rattrappe aussi vite, me rattrappe à la même vitesse, aussi tôt.)

Et tous mes plaisirs sont comme hier, *like Yesterday*, comme l'hier, comme venus d'hier, mes plaisirs sont déjà d'hier, mes plaisirs sont l'hier même, d'avance ils sont datés – et d'hier. D'avance ils ont passé, ils sont passés, déjà passés dépassé, déjà des mémoires de jouissance révolue ou des revenances de plaisir. Mes plaisir présents sont au présent (*are*) des présents d'hier, ils sont hier. Non pas: ils ont été ou ils furent hier, mais ils sont présentement hier. Leur être présent est hier, l'hier.[16]

[I run towards death, I precipitate myself towards death and death comes to meet me just as fast. (I run straight towards death, I run to death (*I run to Death*) and death *comes towards me*, the encounter with death seizes me, captures me or recaptures me just as fast, recaptures me at the same speed, just as soon.)

And all my pleasures are like yesterday, *like Yesterday*, like the yesterday, as if come from yesterday, my pleasures are already from yesterday, my pleasures are yesterday itself, they are dated in advance – and from yesterday. In advance they have passed, they are passed, already passed over, passed beyond [*dépassé*], already memories of lost pleasure or returns, ghosts [*revenances*], of pleasure. My present pleasures are in the present (*are*) yesterday's presents, they are yesterday. Not at all: they have been or they were yesterday, but they are presently yesterday. Their present is yesterday, the yesterday. (J. Hillis Miller, translation)]

And so on. *Und so weiter*. One is tempted to go on and on, quoting the whole six pages. It is hard to find a place to stop. What Derrida writes is so eloquent, so passionate, so clearly inspired by a superb oratorical inspiration such as only the greatest speakers or writers possess, that one wants to have it go on and on. Nor does Derrida just repeat himself. The seven pages turn this way and that the two lines by Donne in a spectacular tour de force that attempts, never quite completely, to exhaust their implications. The sequence ends, seven pages later, with the following sentences. These return, once more, to the theme of doubling, to that echoing 'hier (yesterday)', here repeated eight times in as many lines, to the fear of being haunted by oneself, or of encountering oneself as the wholly other, like meeting over and over that inescapable 'hier':

> Non seulement ce dont je jouis est hier mais peut-être, c'est peut-être *mon* hier ou peut-être l'hier, déjà, aujourd'hui, d'*un autre*, et de toute façon d'un autre, même si c'est déjà, même si ce fut déjà un autre moi-même. Mon plaisir est dès hier, par hier altéré, venu de l'autre, la venue de l'autre.
>
> Et l'autre me dirait, ou je me dirais à l'autre: comme je cours à mort toujours après hier, hier sera toujours à venir: non pas demain, au futur, mais à venir, au-devant, là devant, avant hier.[17]

[Not only what I enjoy is yesterday but perhaps, it is perhaps my yesterday or perhaps the yesterday, already, today, of *another*, and in every way of another, even if it is already, even if it were already another me myself. My pleasure is from yesterday, altered by yesterday, come from the other, the coming of the other [*venu de l'autre, la venue de l'autre*].

And the other would say to me, or I would say to the other, since I always run for dear life [*à mort*] after yesterday, yesterday will always be to come; not tomorrow, in the future, but to come, from in front, there in front, before yesterday [*au-devant, là devant, avant hier*]. (J. Hillis Miller, translation)]

What can one say of the whole sequence, Derrida's spectacular verbal invention initiated by the passage about the 'print of a naked foot'? Though one resists taking Derrida's reflections on death, which run through all ten seminars, as disguised autobiography, it is hard not to see them as premonition of his own death, or as inspired by his fear of death. They were written, it happens, in the months and weeks just before his mortal disease was diagnosed and less than two years before his death. He seems to have known that 'life is so short', as he says, and that he was speeding with ever-increasing rapidity towards death, or that death was rushing towards him. I once, a few years before his death, said to him that I was beginning to think, now and then, about death. With great earnestness, he answered, '*I think about it every day.*' All philosophy, Nietzsche averred, is disguised autobiography. In any case, I can, without hesitation, assert that these seminars are the expression of Derrida's unique version of Heidegger's definition of man (or *Dasein*) as 'Being toward death [*Sein zum Tode*]'.

Derrida emphasises, perhaps even more than Heidegger, the terrifying solitude of one's encounter with death. Only I can die my own death, both Heidegger and Derrida affirm, but Heidegger asserts this relatively dispassionately, as a universal feature of every *Dasein*, whereas Derrida conveys to the reader, as affective passion, by way of what he says about Crusoe, the solitude of being surrounded by death, pursued by death, pursuing death, having death as an immediate tomorrow that is a perpetual yesterday, so that, dying, one is as if always already dead, or an example of the 'living dead (*mort vivant*)'. That phrase he uses repeatedly later, in Seminars Five and Six, both of which are long meditations on facing death. For both Heidegger and Derrida, death is always already interior to *Dasein*. Being towards death is an essential component of my existence as a human being. Nevertheless, for Derrida, death is experienced, at least in part, as not so much inside me as outside, in the form of a quasi-personified being that is rushing towards me to devour me or to bury me alive. Heidegger's phrase, *Sein zum Tode*, suggests that death is always future, something towards which I move, as towards a goal, whereas, for Derrida, death is before, behind, below, above, exterior to me and within me, in whatever temporal or inside/outside direction I look. Derrida, finally, is respectfully dubious about Heidegger's claim that animals cannot die, that only human beings (*Daseins*) can die: *Nur der Mensch stirbt*, says Heidegger. *Das Tier verendet*. Derrida is not so sure about that.

Why all that repetition?

I have spoken so far as if Derrida's reflections on Crusoe's fear of death were purely constative, wholly descriptive, no more than a truthful report of the implications of what Defoe wrote. This is not the case. I shall turn now to an account of how Derrida's words are a peculiar kind of speech act or performative. I have asked what the function is in these seminars of the rhetoric of inexhaustible repetition with a difference. I have compared this linguistic feature to jazz or Bach. Derrida's lectures were notorious for giving their auditors their money's worth, so to speak. His lectures at the various *Cerisy*

Décades devoted to his work went on for six hours, with a break for dinner after three hours. His plenary lectures at a Celan symposium in Seattle and at the Joyce symposium at Frankfort went on for two hours or more and were eventually published as short books. His *Béliers* was written at the same time as the seminars on Defoe and Heidegger.[18] It is a whole book devoted primarily to the reading of just one line from a poem by Paul Celan: *Die Welt is fort, ich muss dich tragen.* This little book is a splendid example of the late Derrida's repetitive late style. The Celan line is cited and commented on more than once in the Defoe/Heidegger seminars, as if he could not get it out of his mind.

How can he go on for so long? Why does he do it? I suggest that Derrida writes this way in order to avoid coming to an end, in more ways than one.

The musical parallel may help to understand this. Derrida's rhetoric of repetition with a difference is like an aria accompanied by orchestra in Bach's *Christmas Oratorio*, for example, the heartbreakingly beautiful alto aria, near the beginning, 'Prepare thyself, Zion (*Bereite dich, Zion*)', in which the same melody is repeated over and over, as if it could never end, until, finally, it leads to the Chorale, 'How shall I receive Thee? (*Wie soll ich dich empfangen?*)'. Or, since Derrida was a jazz buff, his rhetoric is like a jazz structure which repeats the motif and its development with a different instrument or in a wilder and wilder variation, for example a Charlie Parker solo. Just when you think such music must be at an end it starts again, inexhaustibly, with a patience that can be defined as a resistance to coming to the end. If I can just improvise something slightly different, I can go on even longer! In Bach's case, the inexhaustible repetition works as a form of prayer. I must pray incessantly, in the hope that sooner or later God will hear me, and answer my prayer, and that I shall then have prepared myself and be fit to receive Him.

Neither a Charlie Parker solo nor a Derrida improvisation is exactly prayer, though they are not exactly not prayer either. The question of prayer comes up explicitly and is discussed at length later in Derrida's Seminar Eight. The meditation on prayer begins with the characteristic repeated questions with which these seminars often start. For example, early in the first seminar, Derrida asks: '*Qu'est-ce qu'une île? Qu'est une île?*' What exactly is an island? What is an island? No doubt this is a pun on 'île', 'il', island, he. Now, in the eighth seminar, he begins by asking: 'Qu'est-ce que prier? Comment prier? Comment ne pas prier? Plus précisément, si prier consiste à faire quelque chose, en un geste du corps ou un mouvement de l'âme, que fait-on quand on prie? Fait-on quelque chose? (se laisser et se faire prier, développer)?'[19] [What is praying? How to pray? How not to pray? More precisely, if praying consists in doing something, in a gesture of the body or a movement of the soul, what does one do when one prays? Does one do something? (to allow oneself or to make oneself pray, to develop). (J. Hillis Miller, translation).]

The audience will have noticed Derrida's note to himself at the end that promises an even further development in the spoken seminar. This would have been a discussion of the difference between letting oneself pray and making oneself pray. Derrida's questioning initiatory style, the reader can see, is yet another way to avoid getting on with it, or perhaps it is the only way to get on with it, to keep oneself open to the other, and to avoid coming to an end. Bach, Parker and Derrida are all anxious, in the full sense of the word, to avoid doing that – coming to an end.

The first part of the sentence in Celan that Derrida quotes so often, '*Die Welt ist fort* [The world is gone]', is one of Derrida's basic presupposition in these seminars. It is a quite different starting place from Jean-Luc Nancy's or Edmund Husserl's or Heidegger's. All three of the latter, in different ways, see being with others, togetherness, *Mitsein*, as a primordial feature of *Dasein*. That means we all in one way or another share a single world. Heidegger may seem to contradict this claim when he celebrates the way *Dasein* in isolation forms its own world, forms the world, is *Weltbilden*, world-fashioning. That world, my world for me, however, for Heidegger, always, primordially, involves my own particular way of being with others, *Mitsein*. Each *Dasein* is a *Mitsein* or a *Mitdasein* or a *Miteinandersein*. For Derrida, on the contrary, each of us is primordially and forever worldless. Each 'I' turns in a circle within its isolated self, a turning that is a chasing of death and being chased by it. Here is part of what Derrida has to say about Celan's 'Die Welt ist fort':

> ... le monde s'en est allé, déjà, le monde nous a quittés, le monde n'est plus, le monde est au loin, le monde est perdu, le monde est perdu de vue, le monde est hors de vue, le monde est parti, adieu au monde, le monde est décédé, etc.

Mais quel monde? Qu'est-ce que *le* monde? Et, plus tôt ou plus tard: qu'est-ce que *ce* monde-*ci*? Autant de questions inévitables dans toute leur ampleur.[20]

[...the world has gone away, already, the world has left us, the world no longer is, the world is far away, the world is lost, the world is lost to sight, the world is out of sight, the world has departed, farewell to the world, the world is dead, etc.

But what world? What is *the* world? And, sooner or later, what is this world *here*? So many inevitable questions in all their amplitude. (Translation by J. Hillis Miller from file provided by JD)]

I claim that the passage, discussed earlier, commenting on Donne's two lines about his relation to death does not simply paraphrase the lines. It does what it talks about, performatively, that is, it enacts a chasing of death that is a fleeing from death. It does this through words. Derrida's tacit presupposition is that as long as he can go on talking, he is not yet dead.

Derrida has so much to say, and he wants to say it all before it is too late. So he goes on talking, keeping time, in time, 'against time'. Talking, writing philosophy, writing criticism, writing poetry, are different forms of the postponement of death. At the same time, of course, such talking is the incorporation of death within oneself. The words spoken against death, out of mortal fear of death, speak of death, speak death. They anticipate a death that has already come, that is already belated, a thing of the past. I am already living a posthumous life/death. Derrida always already speaks as the late Derrida. He spends his whole life running for dear life (*à mort*) to catch up with death and to escape death.

In these last seminars, the late Derrida makes constant digressions from his announced topics, Defoe and Heidegger. He brings in Donne, Rousseau, Blanchot, Freud, Celan, and so on, in a kind of constant evasion or putting off of coming to the point. *Digression* means getting off the path, getting on a detour, an *Umweg*, or a *Holzweg*. The question of finding the right path, of choosing the right path, is an essential theme of the seminars. The theme is drawn from passages early in the Heidegger seminar of 1929–30, that is, *Die Grundbegriffe*, but also from Crusoe's meditations on which path to choose on his island.

On the one hand, Derrida affirms, no doubt truthfully, that he could make a whole year of seminars on this or that passage he cites, that he will talk of it later, or cannot talk of it now, or has talked about it elsewhere, in a complex rhetoric of evasion, temporising, and postponement. On the other hand, he keeps inserting new material from other authors that prevents him from moving forward on the path he begins by saying he has chosen and that he calls, in the file name of each computer file: 'Hei_Foe.' The sudden insertion of two lines from Donne that, he says, appeared out of nowhere in his memory is such a digression.

Derrida's discourse of digression turns in a round of constant rhetorical iteration, saying the same thing over and over in slightly different ways, often within the same sentence. It might be called an inexhaustible rhetoric of apposition, since it often advances, and does not advance, through a series of phrases in apposition. Here is a small-scale example, a cascade of phrases for being dead: 'quand je serai passé, quand j'aurai passé, quand je serai parti, décédé, éloigné, disparu, absolument sans défense, désarmé, entre leurs mains, c'est-à-dire, comme on dit, pour ainsi dire, mort'[21] [when I will have passed, when I have passed, when I will have departed, deceased, gone away, disappeared, absolutely without defence, disarmed, in their hands, that is to say, to put it that way, dead (J. Hillis Miller, translation)]. This could go on interminably, since there is no reason not to add yet another phrase in apposition, though the passage as written ends with the dead clunk or clank of the word *mort*, death, as if he had finally brought himself, reluctantly, to avoid euphemism. 'Ask not for whom the bell tolls', said John Donne, 'It tolls for thee.'

The passage cited above about Celan's *Die Welt ist fort* is a good example of Derrida's rhetoric of apposition. Derrida proceeds, without proceeding, by a constant process of capping what he has just said, with a still deeper insight, as if he were saying: 'You think that is all I can find to say about this passage I have cited, but you ain't seen nothing yet.' He then proceeds to another higher, even less obvious or less predictable insight, like Charlie Parker transposing a melody to a yet higher harmonic.

Though I don't find this boring, quite the opposite, nevertheless Derrida's linguistic strategy is something like the temporal structure of profound boredom as Heidegger describes it with his example of waiting four hours for the next train in a provincial railroad station, or as when we say, 'I'm bored to death.' Derrida has little to say about the theme of boredom, *Langweile*, in Heidegger's seminars, though the discussion takes up over a hundred pages in *The Fundamental Concepts of Metaphysics*. We want the train to come and we do not want the train to come, since profound boredom, like the fear of death, or like mourning or melancholy, puts us, Heidegger argues, in tune (*Stimmung*) with our authentic *Dasein*, the deepest levels of our being. An analysis of profound boredom will lead us to find the right path for an understanding of 'World, Finitude, Solitude (*Welt – Endlichkeit – Einsamkeit*)', as they are named in the subtitle of Heidegger's seminars. All ten of Derrida's last seminars, as I have said, are governed by the running away from death that is a running towards death. That movement in place has a temporal structure not unlike that of profound boredom as Heidegger describes it.

Derrida's latest seminars constitute an energetic resistance to becoming the late Derrida. This just makes him later than ever, further and further away from his announced goal, like the rabbit in *Alice in Wonderland*. 'Oh dear! Oh dear! I shall be late!' says the rabbit, after taking a watch out of its waistcoat pocket. The white rabbit has to run very fast to stay in the same place. All of us will ultimately be late, really late. To reach the goal, to be on time, would be to be dead, so Derrida keeps talking, not to reach the goal, but to avoid reaching the goal. He must keep being late in order to avoid being late.[22] The later he is the better, until finally he is, alas, on time. The train comes, and he becomes the late Derrida.

Notes

1. J. Derrida, *La Carte postale. De Socrate à Freud et au-delà* (Paris: Flammarion, 1980) [translated A. Bass, *The Post Card: From Socrates to Freud and Beyond* (Chicago: Chicago University Press, 1987)].
2. M. Cervantes, *Exemplary Stories*, trans. L. Lipson (Oxford: OUP, 1998).
3. L. Sterne, *The Life and Opinions of Tristram Shandy, Gentleman* (London: Folio Society, 1970).
4. D. Defoe, *Robinson Crusoe*, introduction by V. Woolf (New York: The Modern Library, 2001) 142.
5. Ibid., 145–6.
6. J. Derrida, 'La bête et le souverain (deuxième année)', Seminars of 2002–3. Personal computer files.

7. G. Poulet, *Études sur le temps humain*, Vols. I–IV (Paris: Plon, 1949–68).
8. P. B. Shelley, *Poetical Works*, ed. T. Hutchinson (Oxford: OUP, 1978).
9. W. Kelly, *Pogo: 'We Have Met the Enemy and He is Us'* (New York: Simon & Schuster, 1972).
10. T. Morrison, *Beloved* (New York: Alfred A. Knopf, 1988).
11. A. Rimbaud, *Oeuvres Complètes* (Paris: Gallimard, 1972) 249–50.
12. S. Freud, 'Delusions and Dreams' in Jensen's *Gradiva*, in J. Strachey et al., trans., *The Standard Edition of the Complete Psychological Works* (London: Hogarth Press, 1953–74), Vol. IX, pp. 7–93.
13. M. Heidegger, *Die Grundbegriffe der Metaphysik: Welt – Endlichkeit – Einsamkeit*, Gesamtausgabe bd. 29–30 (Frankfurt a.m.: Vittorio Klostermann, 1983) [trans. W. McNeill and N. Walker, *The Fundamental Concepts of Metaphysics: World, Finitude, Solitude* (Indianapolis: Indiana University Press, 1995)].
14. Derrida, 'La bête et le souverain (deuxième année)'.
15. J. Donne, *The Divine Poems*, ed. H. Gardner (Oxford: Clarendon Press, 1978) 12.
16. Derrida, 'La bête et le souverain (deuxième année)'.
17. Derrida, 'La bête et le souverain (deuxième année)'.
18. J. Derrida, *Béliers. Le dialogue ininterrompu: Entre deux infinis, le poème* (Paris: Galilée, 2003) [trans. T. Dutoit and P. Romanski under the title, 'Rams. Uninterrupted Dialogue – Between Two Infinities, the Poem', in J. Derrida, *Sovereignties in Question – The Poetics of Paul Celan* (New York: Fordham University Press, 2005) 135–63.
19. Derrida, 'La bête et le souverain (deuxième année)'.
20. Derrida, *Béliers*, pp. 46–7.
21. Derrida, 'La bête et le souverain (deuxième année)'.
22. Derrida's formulations, both for and against Gadamer's description of hermeneutics as a '*processus infini*' (*Béliers*, p. 38), about the inexhaustibility of interpretation and its uncertainty, are the theoretical expression of this as a principle of responsible reading, reading as a response to the otherness of the text:

Cette analyse formelle [that Gadamer exemplifies] peut aller très loin. Elle le doit. Mais elle paraît peu risquée. Elle appartient à l'ordre de l'assurance calculable et des évidences décidables. Il n'en va plus même pour la réponse herméneutique à l'*Anspruch* du poème ou dans le dialogue intérrieur du lecteur ou du contre-signataire. Cette réponse, cette responsabilité, peut se poursuivre à l'infini, de façon ininterrompue, elle va du sense au sens, de vérité en vérité, sans autre loi calculable que celle que lui assignent la letter et le dispositif formel du poème. Mais quoique surveillée par la même loi, à jamais assujettie à elle, tout aussi responsible, l'expérience que j'appelle disséminale fait et assume, à travers le moment herméneutique même, à meme l'herméneutique, l'épreuve d'une interruption, d'une césure ou d'une ellipse, d'une entame. Telle béance n'appartient ni au sens, ni au phénomène, ni à la vérité mais, les rendant possible en leur restance, elle marque dans le poème le hiatus d'une blessure dont les lèvres ne se ferment ou ne se rassemblent jamais. (*Béliers*, p. 54)

This formal analysis [that Gadamer exemplifies] can go very far. It must. Yet it appears of little risk. It belongs to the order of a calculable undertaking and of decidable evidence. It doesn't even work for the hermeneutical response to the *Anspruch* of the poem or in the interior dialogue of the reader or counter-signatory. This response, this responsibility can be pursued to infinity, in uninterrupted fashion, going from meaning to meaning, from truth to truth without a calculable law other than that which the letter and the formal device of the poem assign to it. Yet even though supervised by the same law, forever subjected to it, every bit as responsible, the experience that I call disseminal undergoes and shoulders, across the hermeneutic moment itself, flush with hermeneutics, the test of an interruption, of a caesura or of an ellipsis, of an inaugural cut. Such a gaping belongs neither to meaning, to the phenomenon, nor to truth, but, by making them possible in their remaindering, it marks in the poem the hiatus of a wound the lips of which will never come to close, never gather together. [From translation file supplied by JD, slightly altered.] [Derrida, 'Rams', op. cit., 152–3.]

Index